**B 1** Finde die Länder und Kontinente und schreib sie auf.

1 KREFRANICH _Frankreich_

5 STRANEILAU _____

2 DNANELG _England_

6 LATOSCHTDN _Schottland_

7 ENLAITI _Italien_

3 ENSAI _Asien_

8 AKFARI _Afrika_

4 SCHTUDENALD _Deutschland_

**B 2** Wer ist wohin gefahren? Hör gut zu und verbinde die passenden Namen und Länder.

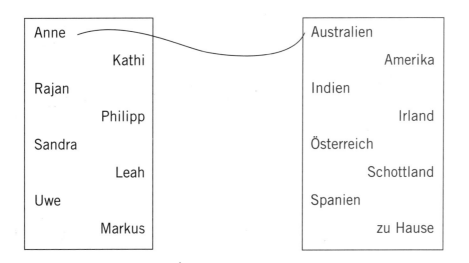

**C** Wohin sind sie im Sommer gefahren? Füll die Sprechblasen aus.

a

Wir sind **nach** Amerika geflogen.

b

Ich bin _____ Spanien
_____ .

c

Wir sind _____ _____
_____ .

d

Ich _____ _____ _____
_____ .

**D**  Wohin bist du im Sommer gefahren? Macht Dialoge mit den Bildern.

*Beispiel:*

A   *Wohin bist du im Sommer gefahren?*

B   *Ich bin nach Frankreich gefahren.*

**E** Du bist dran! Wohin bist du im Sommer gefahren?

_____

_____

_____

_____

# Wie waren die Ferien?

## A1 🔊 Hör gut zu und sing mit!

### Spanien

Ich bin nach Spanien geflogen
Wohin bist du geflogen?
Ich bin nach Spanien geflogen
Und es war toll, toll, toll!

Sonne, Schwimmen, Sport und Strand,
Spanien ist mein Lieblingsland!

Ich bin zwei Wochen geblieben
Wie lange bist du geblieben?
Ich bin zwei Wochen geblieben
Und es war schön, schön, schön!

*Refrain*

Ich hab' Paella gegessen
Was hast du gegessen?
Ich hab' Paella gegessen
Und es war gut, gut, gut!

*Refrain*

Ich bin zum Strand gefahren
Wohin bist du gefahren?
Ich bin zum Strand gefahren
Und es war heiß, heiß, heiß!

*Refrain*

Ich bin nach Hause geflogen
Wohin bist du geflogen?
Ich bin nach Hause geflogen
Und es war schade, schade, schade!

*Refrain*

## A2 Finde die passenden Bilder und Antworten.

**1** „Ich bin nach Spanien geflogen." Das ist Bild ...

**a**  □

**b**   ✓

**2** „Sonne, Schwimmen, Sport und Strand ..." Was ist Sonne?

**a**  ✓  **b**  □

**3** „Ich bin zwei Wochen geblieben" – was heißt das?

**a** I stayed for two weeks. ✓

**b** I went home for two weeks. □

**4** „Ich habe Paella gegessen." Das ist Bild ...

**a**  □  **b**  ✓

**5** „Es war heiß" – wie ist das?

**a**  ✓  **b**   □

**6** „Es war schade" – was heißt das?

**a** Ich bin gern nach Hause geflogen. □

**b** Ich bin nicht gern nach Hause geflogen. □

# How to use your *Arbeitsheft*

## Welcome to the *Klasse! 2 Arbeitsheft*

This *Arbeitsheft* is designed to help you practise German. A yellow and green arrow in your *Lehrbuch* tells you which activity to go to in your *Arbeitsheft*.

**D** ▶ = go to activity D in the corresponding unit in your *Arbeitsheft*.

The symbols below are in the *Lehrbuch* and in your *Arbeitsheft*:

[◉] listen to the cassette with this activity

[👥] work with a partner

[👥] work in a group

[W📖] use a dictionary

**E2 Du bist dran!**

Wherever you see this panel, you will be able to write down information about yourself, in German. By the end of the *Arbeitsheft* you will have built up a bank of German phrases all about yourself which you can use in future writing tasks.

| Can you …? | Listening | Speaking | Reading | Writing |
|---|---|---|---|---|
|  |  |  |  |  |
|  |  |  |  |  |

At the end of every unit you will find a checklist of everything you have learnt. You will be able to tick these off once you have completed certain activities in your *Lehrbuch* – your teacher will tell you which.

To help you understand the activities in this book, there is a list of instructions on page 95.

**F**  **Was haben sie gemacht? Finde die Sätze.**

1  Ich habe meinen Brieffreund         **a**  gegessen.

2  Wir haben einen Ausflug         **b**  gefahren.

3  Ich habe Pizza         **c**  besucht.

4  Wir haben die Stadt         **d**  getrunken.

5  Ich habe Cola         **e**  gemacht.

6  Wir sind zum Strand         **f**  besichtigt.

**G**  Was hat Jasmin in Marseille gemacht?
**Hör gut zu und finde die passenden Bilder.**

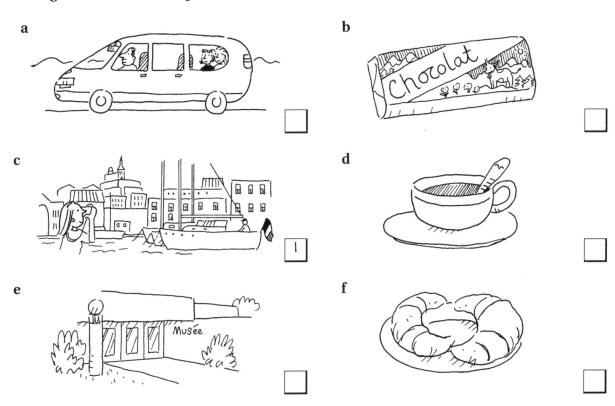

**H**  Was haben sie gemacht? Hör gut zu und kreuz die passenden Bilder an.

|  |  |  |  |  |  |  |  |  |
|---|---|---|---|---|---|---|---|---|
| Tanja |  |  |  | ✗ | ✗ |  |  |  |
| Alex |  |  |  |  |  |  |  |  |
| Silke |  |  |  |  |  |  |  |  |
| Rainer |  |  |  |  |  |  |  |  |

## I1 Lies Maikes Postkarte und füll die Lücken aus.

Hallo Tom!

Viele Grüße aus England. Ich bin am Samstag nach Manchester _____.
Ich habe meine Brieffreundin Sarah _____. Sarah ist sehr nett! Wir
haben viel gemacht: wir haben Fußball _____ und wir haben auch
einen Ausflug _____. Ich habe auch Fisch _____ und viel
Tee _____. Ich habe auch die Stadt _____ –
Manchester ist sehr schön! Und ich habe Souvenirs _____. Am Sonntag
sind wir ins Schwimmbad _____.

Tschüs!

Maike

getrunken

gefahren

gespielt

gegangen

besichtigt

gemacht

gegessen

besucht

gekauft

## I2 Du bist dran! Schreib eine Postkarte (so wie Maike) mit den Bildern und den Perfekt-Partizipien (Wörtern) von Übung I1.

1  2  3  4

5  6  7  8

1  Ich bin _____

2  Ich habe _____

3  Wir haben _____

4  Ich habe auch _____

5  und wir haben _____

6  Ich habe _____

7  Ich habe auch _____

8  und wir sind _____

**J** Du bist dran! Was hast du in den Ferien gemacht?
Nimm die Informationen auf Kassette auf.

*Beispiel:*

*Ich bin im Sommer nach Deutschland geflogen. Ich habe viel gemacht: Ich habe ...*

_____

_____

**K** Wetter-Worträtsel. Schreib die Sätze richtig auf.

ESWARSEHRSCHLECHTESHATVIELGESCHNEITESWARSEHRSONNIGESWARIMMERWOLKIG

1  _____

2  _____

3  _____

4  _____

**L** Wie war das Wetter? Finde die passenden Bilder.

1 Es hat viel geregnet. ☐     4 Es war sehr heiß. ☐

2 Es war wolkig. ☐     5 Es war immer kalt. ☐

3 Es war windig. ☐     6 Es war neblig. ☐

a      b

c     d

e     f

**M** Schau die Wetterkarte an. Richtig oder falsch? Schreib ✓ oder ✗
und korrigiere dann die falschen Sätze.

| Stadt | Wetter | Richtig/ Falsch? | Richtige Sätze |
|-------|--------|------------------|----------------|
| Hamburg | Es war sonnig. | | |
| Berlin | Es war heiß. | | |
| Dresden | Es war neblig. | | |
| Köln | Es war windig. | | |
| Stuttgart | Es hat geschneit. | | |
| München | Es war schön. | | |

**N** „Wo warst du – und wie war das Wetter?" Macht Dialoge mit den Bildern.

*Beispiel*:

**A** *Wo warst du in den Ferien?*

**B** *Ich war in Österreich.*

**A** *Wie war das Wetter?*

**B** *Es war sehr windig!*

O   **Wo haben sie gewohnt? Schreib die passenden Wörter auf.**

1

2

3

bei

**1** G
A
S
T
F
A
M
**2** F e r i e n w o h n u n g
I
L
I
E

**3**

**4** Z e l t

**5** F r e u n d e n

**6** H o t e l

**7** W o h n m o b i l

**8**

4

5

6

7

8

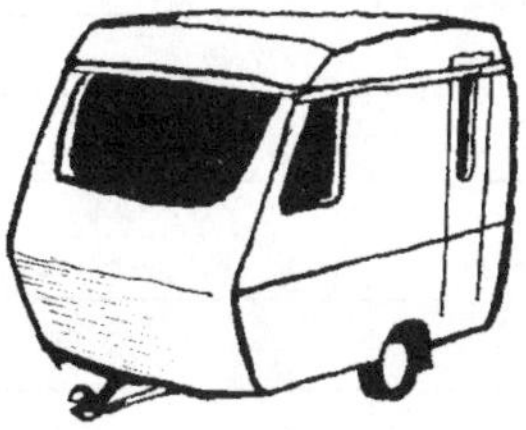

**P1 Wo haben sie gewohnt? Finde die passenden Bilder.**

1 Ich habe bei Freunden gewohnt. <u>d</u>

2 Ich habe in einem Wohnmobil gewohnt. <u>c</u>

3 Ich habe in einem Hotel gewohnt. <u>a</u>

4 Ich habe in einer Ferienwohnung gewohnt. <u>b</u>

a

b

c

d

**P2** Hör gut zu und füll die Lücken aus.

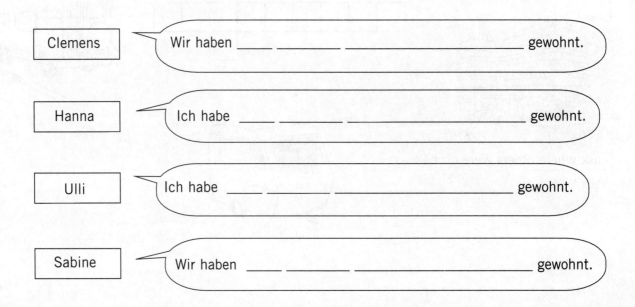

Clemens | Wir haben _____ _____ _____ gewohnt.

Hanna | Ich habe _____ _____ gewohnt.

Ulli | Ich habe _____ _____ _____ gewohnt.

Sabine | Wir haben _____ _____ gewohnt.

**Q** Wo hat Sven in Florida gewohnt? Wie war alles? Schreib Sprechblasen.

Ich habe in einem Hotel gewohnt. Das Hotel war sehr laut.

| Can you ...? | Listening | Speaking | Reading | Writing |
|---|---|---|---|---|
| say where you went on holiday | | | | |
| ask others where they went on holiday | | | | |
| ask what others did on holiday | | | | |
| say what you did on holiday | | | | |
| ask where others were on holiday | | | | |
| say where you were on holiday | | | | |
| ask what the weather was like on holiday | | | | |
| say what the weather was like on holiday | | | | |
| ask where someone stayed on holiday | | | | |
| say where you stayed on holiday | | | | |
| describe your accommodation | | | | |

# Mein Alltag

## A 1  Hör gut zu und sing mit!

### *Mein Tag beginnt*

*Ich stehe auf!*
*Ich stehe auf!*
*Es ist sieben Uhr*
*Und ich steh' auf!*

*Ich wasche mich!*
*Ich wasche mich!*
*Es ist Viertel nach*
*Und ich wasche mich!*

*Ich ziehe mich an!*
*Ich ziehe mich an!*
*Es ist fast halb acht*
*Und ich zieh' mich an!*

*Ich esse Toast!*
*Ich esse Toast!*
*Es ist Viertel vor*
*Und ich esse Toast!*

*Ich trinke Milch!*
*Ich trinke Milch!*
*Es ist zehn vor acht*
*Und ich trinke Milch!*

*Mein Tag beginnt!*
*Mein Tag beginnt!*
*Es ist schon acht Uhr*
*Und mein Tag beginnt!*

## A 2 Finde die passenden Bilder und Antworten.

1 „Ich stehe auf." Das ist Bild ...

a  ☐　　b  ☑

2 Wie spät ist es? Schreib die Uhrzeit auf.

a Es ist Viertel nach sieben.  `__:__`

b Es ist halb acht.  `07:30`

3 „Ich wasche mich" – was heißt das?

a I am washing up. ☐

b I have a wash. ☑

4 „Ich esse Toast." Und du? Was isst du zum Frühstück?

_____

_____

5 „Ich trinke Milch." Was ist das?

a  ☑　　b  ☐

6 „Mein Tag beginnt" – was heißt das?

a Ich gehe jetzt in die Schule. ☐

b Schule ist fertig! Ich gehe nach Hause. ☐

**B 1** **Was machen sie? Finde die passenden Bilder.**

1 Ich stehe auf. — *c*

2 Ich wasche mich. — *f*

3 Ich ziehe mich an. — *e*

4 Ich gehe in die Schule. — *b*

5 Ich frühstücke. — *h*

6 Ich gehe nach Hause. — *d*

7 Ich ziehe mich aus. — *g*

8 Ich gehe ins Bett. — *a*

a    b

c    d

e    f

g    h

**B 2** Wer sagt was? Hör gut zu und finde die passenden Bilder in Übung B1.

1 Peter — *c*

2 Uwe

3 Kai

4 Anne

5 Philipp

6 Leah

7 Hanna

8 Monika

**B 3** **A sagt einen Satz von Übung B1, B macht eine Pantomime.**

*Beispiel:*

Ich wasche mich.

Richtig!

**C1** Was fehlt? Füll die Lücken aus und finde die passenden Bilder.

1  I_h __as_ _e mi__ __ .  □  a

2  __ __h z_e_e m__h a_. □

3  I_ __ _i_h_ m_c_ a_s. □  c

**C2**  Ist alles richtig? A fragt, B antwortet. Dann ist B dran.

*Beispiel:*

*A Was machst du in Bild a?*

*B Ich ...*

**D**  Wann machst du das? Hör gut zu und schreib die Namen unter die passenden Bilder.

a

c

e

b

d

_____

_____Angi_____

_____

| Oma |
| Britta |
| Angi |
| Martin |
| Ralf |

**E**  Was machst du – und wann? Schreib Sätze.

a

b

_Um halb sieben stehe ich auf._  _____

c

d

e

_____  _____  _____

**F** Wie hilfst du zu Hause? Füll die Lücken aus.

1

2

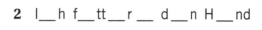

3   4  5

6   7

1 __ch  s__  __g__  St__  __b.

2 I__h  f__tt__r  __  d__n  H__nd

__nd  d__  __  K__tz__.

3 Ich  r__  __m__  m__  __n  Z__mm__r  a__f.

4 __  __h  p__tz__  d__s

B__d__z__mm__  r.

5 Ich  d__ck__  d__n  T__sch.

6 __c__  k__  __f__  __  __n.

7 __ch  w__sch__  __b.

**G** Finde die passenden Wörter und schreib die Sätze auf.

1 Ich stehe [ ]    a ein.    1 _____

2 Ich kaufe [ ]    b auf.    2 _____

3 Ich räume [ ]    c ab.     3 _____

4 Ich wasche [ ]   d Staub.  4 _____

5 Ich sauge [ ]    e auf.    5 _____

**H1** [📼] Wie oft hilft Martin zu Hause? Hör gut zu und füll die Tabelle aus.

| immer = ✔✔✔✔ | einmal pro Woche = ✔ |
| jeden Tag = ✔✔✔ | selten = ✗ |
| oft = ✔✔ | nie = ✗✗ |

| | | | | | | |
|---|---|---|---|---|---|---|
| | ✔✔✔ | | | | | |

**H2** **Schreib Sprechblasen für Martin. Was sagt er?**

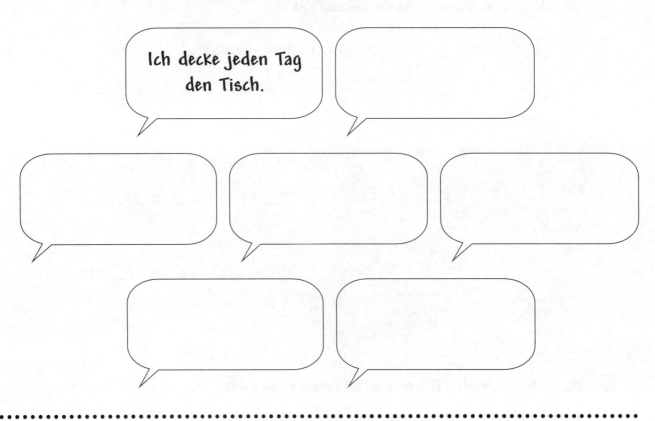

Ich decke jeden Tag den Tisch.

**I** **Du bist dran! Wie hilfst du zu Hause? Wie oft machst du das?**

_____

_____

_____

_____

_____

_____

**J** **Jasmin hilft zu Hause. Was fehlt? Füll die Lücken aus.**

1 Ich füttere die _____ .

2 Ich decke den _____ .

3 Ich räume das _____ auf.

4 Ich putze das _____ .

5 Ich füttere den _____ .

6 Ich wasche das _____ .

| Auto |
| Katze |
| Badezimmer |
| Hund |
| Tisch |
| Zimmer |

**K** Was sagen sie? Schreib die Sätze richtig auf.

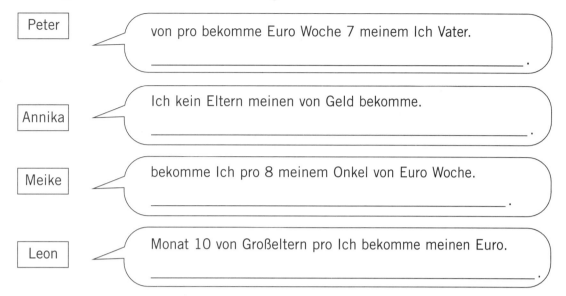

Peter

von pro bekomme Euro Woche 7 meinem Ich Vater.

_____.

Annika

Ich kein Eltern meinen von Geld bekomme.

_____.

Meike

bekomme Ich pro 8 meinem Onkel von Euro Woche.

_____.

Leon

Monat 10 von Großeltern pro Ich bekomme meinen Euro.

_____.

**L** Von wem bekommst du Geld? Füll die Lücken aus.

1 Von m _____ Großeltern.   4 Von m _____ Opa.

2 Von m _____ Stiefvater.   5 Von m _____ Tante.

3 Von m _____ Oma.   6 Von m _____ Onkel.

**M** Klaus hat eine Umfrage gemacht. Hier sind die Resultate. Was sagen
die Schüler und Schülerinnen? Schreib Sprechblasen.

| | Susie | Heiko | Kai | Kathi | Philipp |
|---|---|---|---|---|---|
| Wie viel? | € 5 | € 30 | € 3 | € 20 | € 2 |
| Von wem? | Tante | Eltern | Großeltern | Stiefmutter | Vater |
| Wie oft? | 1 × Woche | 1 × Monat | jeden Tag | 1 × Monat | jeden Tag |

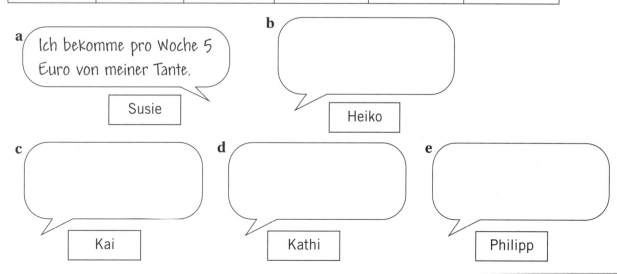

a Ich bekomme pro Woche 5 Euro von meiner Tante.

Susie

b

Heiko

c

Kai

d

Kathi

e

Philipp

**N** **Was kaufst du? Finde die passenden Wörter.**

| ein Fahrrad | Süßigkeiten | eine Stereoanlage | ein Computerspiel | Zeitschriften |
| CDs | Kleidung | Make-up | eine Jeans | einen Computer |

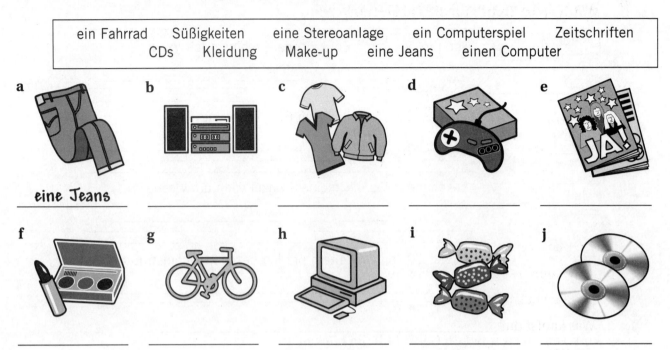

a
_eine Jeans_

b

c

d

e

f

g

h

i

j

**O1** 🔊 **Hör gut zu und verbinde die Namen mit den passenden Bildern.**

Ich kaufe ...                    Ich spare für ...

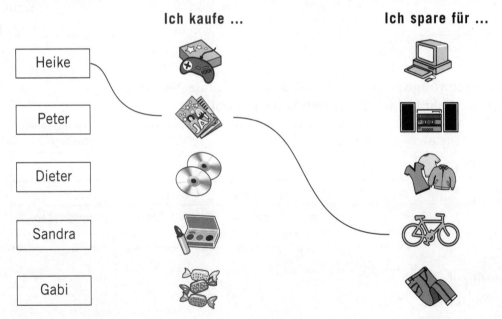

Heike

Peter

Dieter

Sandra

Gabi

**O2 Was sagen sie in Übung O1? Schreib die Sätze auf.**

1 Heike   _Ich kaufe Zeitschriften und ich spare für ein Fahrrad._

2 Peter   _____

3 Dieter  _____

4 Sandra  _____

5 Gabi    _____

**P** **Wofür spart Tom? Füll die Lücken aus.**

Ich spare für …

e _____ Computer.

e _____ Computerspiel.

e _____ Jeans.

e _____ Buch.

Ich spare für …

e _____ Fahrrad.

e _____ Stereoanlage.

e _____ Pullover.

e _____ Auto.

**Q** **Du bist dran!**

Von wem bekommst du dein Geld?_____

Wie viel bekommst du? _____

Was kaufst du? _____

Wofür sparst du? _____

**R 1** **Was für Nebenjobs haben Sven und Jasmin? Lies die Sätze und finde die passenden Bilder.**

Sven

**1** Ich wasche das Auto. ☐

**2** Ich führe den Hund aus. ☐

**3** Ich helfe zu Hause. ☐

a   b   c

Jasmin

**4** Ich arbeite im Garten. ☐

**5** Ich bin Babysitterin. ☐

**6** Ich trage Zeitungen aus. ☐

d   e   f

**R 2** **„Hast du einen Nebenjob?" Mach eine Umfrage in deiner Klasse und schreib die Resultate auf. Frag vier Schüler/Schülerinnen.**

*Beispiel:*

*A   Hast du einen Nebenjob, Philip?*

*B   Ja, ich helfe zu Hause und ich trage Zeitungen aus.*

Philip: Ich helfe zu Hause und ich trage Zeitungen aus.

**1** _____

**2** _____

**3** _____

**4** _____

**S** 👥 **Würfelspiel: Wie viel verdienst du? Wie oft bekommst du das?**
**A fragt, B antwortet. Dann ist B dran.**

*Beispiel:*

**A** *Wie viel verdienst du?*

**B** *Zwei und drei! Ich verdiene pro Tag zwanzig Euro.*

⊡ **€15**   ⊡ **€20**

⊡ **€6**   ⊡ **€17**

⊡ **€35**   ⊡ **€4**

---

**T**   **Du bist dran!**

Hast du einen Nebenjob? _____

_____

Wie viel verdienst du und wie oft? _____

_____

**U 1 Was ist positiv und was ist negativ? Schreib zwei Listen.**

| Ich mag den Job.   Ich finde den Job langweilig.   Ich finde den Job toll. |
| Das macht Spaß!   Der Job ist schrecklich.   Der Job ist super.   Das finde ich gut. |
| Das macht keinen Spaß!   Das mag ich gar nicht. |
| Der Manager ist sehr unfreundlich.   Ich mag den Job sehr gern. |
| Ich finde den Job nicht so gut. |

| **Positiv** | **Negativ** |
|---|---|
| Ich mag den Job. | Ich finde den Job langweilig. |
|  |  |
|  |  |
|  |  |
|  |  |
|  |  |

## U2  Positiv oder negativ – was ist deine Meinung? Macht Dialoge.

**Beispiel:**

A  *Hast du einen Nebenjob?*

B  *Ja, ich wasche das Auto.*

A  *Und wie findest du den Job?*

B  *Ich finde den Job super. Das macht Spaß!*

a    macht Spaß

b    langweilig

c    toll

d  macht Spaß

e  schrecklich

f    gut

d  mag nicht gern

e  schrecklich

f  gut

## V  Lies die Postkarte und schreib eine Antwort-Postkarte.

**Beschreib:**
- deinen Nebenjob
- wie viel du verdienst
- was du kaufst
- wofür du sparst
- wie du den Job findest.

> Hallo!
> Wie geht's? Ich habe einen Nebenjob – ich finde den Job toll! Ich arbeite für meine Großeltern im Garten. Ich arbeite einmal pro Woche und ich verdiene 10 Euro 50 Cent. Ich kaufe Zeitschriften und Süßigkeiten, aber ich spare auch für ein neues Computerspiel. Hast du einen Nebenjob?
> Schreib bald wieder!
>
> Martina

| Can you …? | Listening | Speaking | Reading | Writing |
|---|---|---|---|---|
| describe your daily routine | | | | |
| say what you do at specific times | | | | |
| ask others how they help around the house | | | | |
| say how you help around the house | | | | |
| say how much pocket money you get, how often and from whom | | | | |
| say what you buy with your money | | | | |
| say how much you save and what you are saving for | | | | |
| describe part time jobs | | | | |
| ask others whether they have a part time job | | | | |
| say how much money you earn | | | | |
| express opinions about your part time job | | | | |

# Freunde und Familie

## A 1 🔊 Hör gut zu und sing mit!

### Mein bester Freund

*Lukas ist mein bester Freund*
*Bester Freund, bester Freund*
*Lukas ist der beste Freund*
*Der beste Freund der Welt*

*Er hat blaue Augen*
*Er hat blaue Augen*
*Er hat blaue Augen*
*Lukas ist so lieb*

**Refrain**

*Er hat rote Haare*
*Er hat rote Haare*
*Er hat rote Haare*
*Lukas ist so lieb*

**Refrain**

*Er trägt eine Brille*
*Er trägt eine Brille*
*Er trägt eine Brille*
*Lukas ist so lieb*

**Refrain**

*Er ist immer lustig*
*Er ist immer lustig*
*Er ist immer lustig*
*Lukas ist so lieb*

**Refrain**

## A2 Finde die passenden Antworten.

1 „Lukas ist mein bester Freund." Was heißt das?

  **a** Lukas ist mein Freund Nummer eins. ☐

  **b** Lukas ist nicht mein Freund. ☐

2 „Lukas ist so lieb." Wie ist er?

  **a** Er ist nie frech. ☐

  **b** Er ist immer frech. ☐

3 „Er hat rote Haare." Was heißt das?

  **a** He's got blue eyes. ☐

  **b** He's got red hair. ☐

4 „Er trägt eine Brille." Was heißt das auf Englisch?

  **a** He's wearing glasses. ☐

  **b** He's wearing an earring. ☐

5 Zeichne Lukas und male das Bild aus.

**Lukas**

**B** Schreib die Sätze richtig auf.

1 Freundin Tanja beste Meine heißt . _____

2 sind Haare Seine braun . _____

3 Augen Ich blaue habe . _____

4 aus siehst du Wie ? _____

5 trage Ich Ohrring einen . _____

6 blonde Sie Haare hat . _____

**C** Wer ist das? Finde die passenden Bilder.

1 Ich trage eine Brille. ☐

2 Ich habe braune Augen und schwarze Haare. ☐

3 Meine Haare sind blond und lang. ☐

4 Ich trage Ohrringe. ☐

5 Ich habe kurze lockige Haare. ☐

a b c d e

**D 1**  „Wie siehst du aus?" Hör gut zu und zeichne Lukas, Maja und Alexander. Schreib auch die passenden Farben für sie auf.

Lukas

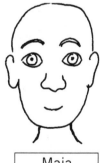
Maja

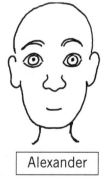
Alexander

| braun |
| rot |
| grün |
| blond |
| blau |

Haare: **rot** _____

Augen: _____

Haare: _____

Augen: _____

Haare: _____

Augen: _____

**D 2** Ratespiel – wer ist das? A wählt ein Bild und beschreibt es, B rät.
Dann ist B dran.

*Beispiel:*

**A** *Er hat rote Haare. Seine Augen sind …*

**B** *Das ist Lukas!*

**D 3** „Was ist deine Lieblings …?" Was sagen Lukas, Maja und Alexander?
Hör gut zu und schreib *L*, *M* oder *A* auf.

a

b

c

d

e

f

**D4** Was ist deine Lieblings … ? Schreib Sprechblasen für Lukas, Maja und Alexander.

*Beispiel:* *Meine Lieblingsfarbe ist … und meine Lieblingsgruppe ist …*

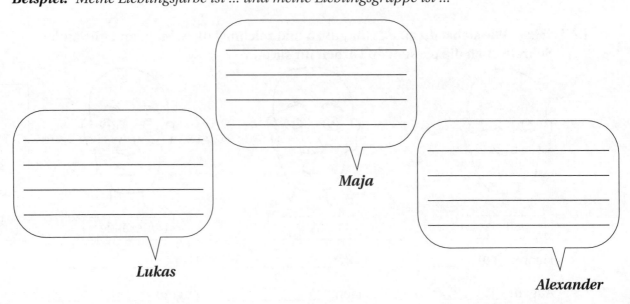

Maja

Lukas

Alexander

**E** Finde Fotos – z.B. von Freunden, Freundinnen, Film-, Pop- oder Sportstars usw.
Wähle ein Foto und kleb es auf. Wie sieht die Person aus? Beschreib sie oder ihn.

Foto

_____

_____

_____

_____

_____

_____

_____

_____

_____

_____

_____

**F** Lies Jans Brief und die Sätze unten. Sind sie richtig (✔) oder falsch (✗)?
Korrigiere die falschen Sätze.

> Ja, wie sehe ich aus? Also, ich habe kurze braune
> Haare. Meine Haare sind lockig. Und du - wie siehst du
> aus? Hast du auch braune Haare? Oder sind deine Haare
> blond oder rot? Oder schwarz? Meine Augen - meine
> Augen sind blau. Ich trage auch eine Brille, aber ich
> trage keinen Ohrring. Ja, und was ist meine
> Lieblingsfarbe? Grün, Gelb - oder Orange? Nein, meine
> Lieblingsfarbe ist Schwarz. Was ist deine Lieblings-
> musik? Hörst du gern Hip-Hop und Rap? Also, ich finde
> Rap sehr gut, aber meine Lieblingsmusik ist Techno.

|  | Richtig/Falsch | Richtige Sätze |
|---|---|---|
| **1** Jans Haare sind blond und kurz. | | |
| **2** Er hat glatte Haare. | | |
| **3** Er hat braune Augen. | | |
| **4** Er trägt einen Ohrring. | | |
| **5** Er mag Orange. | | |
| **6** Er hört am liebsten Rap. | | |

**G**  Du bist dran! Wie siehst du aus? Was ist deine Lieblingsfarbe, -musik oder -gruppe?
Was ist dein Lieblingsfilm? Finde ein Foto von dir und beschreib dich.

_____

_____

_____

_____

Foto

**H1**  Wie bist du? Finde 12 Adjektive im Worträtsel und schreib sie unten auf Deutsch auf.

**H2**  [W] Wie heißt das auf Englisch? Finde die passenden Wörter
im Wörterbuch und schreib sie auf.

| U | L | U | S | T | I | G | J | V |
|---|---|---|---|---|---|---|---|---|
| N | A | R | R | O | G | A | N | T |
| F | R | E | C | H | I | K | S | S |
| R | L | C | A | G | D | U | C | Y |
| E | A | L | P | A | L | F | H | M |
| U | U | K | R | Z | U | R | Ü | P |
| N | N | G | T | K | D | E | C | A |
| D | I | D | B | S | E | U | H | T |
| L | S | A | T | I | G | N | T | H |
| I | C | G | E | H | N | D | E | I |
| C | H | B | C | K | U | L | R | S |
| H | S | G | E | M | E | I | N | C |
| L | I | E | B | G | Y | C | R | H |
| N | E | T | T | I | S | H | H | N |

**Deutsch**          **Englisch**

_____     _____

_____     _____

_____     _____

_____     _____

_____     _____

_____     _____

_____     _____

_____     _____

**I 1** 🔊 Wie sind Doro und Uwe? Hör gut zu und schreib die passenden Adjektive in Übung I2 auf.

| | | | |
|---|---|---|---|
| arrogant | frech | freundlich | gemein |
| launisch | lieb | lustig | nett | schüchtern |
| sympathisch | unfreundlich | ungeduldig | |

**I 2** 🔊 Wie oft sind sie das? Hör noch einmal zu und schreib die passenden Buchstaben in die Kästchen.

| **a** immer | **b** oft | **c** manchmal | **d** selten | **e** nie |
|---|---|---|---|---|

| **Doro** | | **Uwe** | |
|---|---|---|---|
| sympathisch | a | | |
| | | | |
| | | | |
| | | | |
| | | | |
| | | | |

**J 1** Lies noch einmal die Wörter in Übung I. Was meinst du – wie ist ein Superfreund/eine Superfreundin? Wie ist er/sie nicht? Schreib Sätze.

*Beispiel:*

*Er ist immer nett.*

*Sie ist nie gemein.*

_____

_____

_____

_____

_____

**J 2**  Ratespiel – wie ist dein Superfreund/deine Superfreundin?
A fragt, B antwortet. Dann ist B dran.

*Beispiel:*

**A**  *Wie ist deine Superfreundin? Ist sie immer frech?*

**B**  *Nein, sie ist immer lieb.*

**A**  *Und wie ist sie nie? Ist sie nie launisch?*

**B**  *Nein, sie ist ...*

**K 1**  „Ich mag ..., weil ...“ Schreib die Sätze richtig auf.

*Beispiel:*

**1**  *Ich mag Tom, weil er nett ist.*

**1**  Ich mag Tom, | weil | nett | ist | er | . | _____

**2**  Ich mag Ina, | weil | ist | sympathisch | sie | . | _____

**3**  Ich mag Mark, | weil | ist | er | freundlich | . | _____

**4**  Ich mag Susi, | weil | lustig | sie | ist | . | _____

**5**  | weil | Max, | Ich | er | schüchtern | mag | ist | . | _____

**6**  | Ich | lieb | sie | Kathi, | weil | ist | mag | . | _____

**K 2**  Schreib Sätze mit „Ich mag ..., weil ...“

*Beispiel:*

**1**  *Ich mag Heiko, weil er nie launisch ist.*

**1**  Heiko – nie launisch _____

**2**  Ulla – selten ungeduldig _____

**3**  Martin – selten arrogant _____

**4**  Cora – nie unfreundlich _____

**5**  Ralf – oft frech _____

**6**  Lola – nie gemein _____

**L** 👥👥 „Wie ist er/sie?" Schreibt Informationen, z.B. für Freunde, Popstars, Sportstars usw. Macht dann Dialoge mit „Ich mag …, weil …"

*Beispiel:*
*Jordan ist immer lustig.*
*Charlotte ist nie …*

**A**   *Ich mag Jordan, weil er immer lustig ist. Und du?*

**B**   *Ich mag Charlotte, weil sie nie …*

**M**   🔊 Annika beschreibt ihre Eltern. Wie sind sie? Hör gut zu und kreuz die passenden Wörter an.

|  | launisch | lieb | lustig | modern | nett | streng | tolerant | altmodisch | ungeduldig |
|---|---|---|---|---|---|---|---|---|---|
| Mutter |  |  |  |  |  |  |  |  |  |
| Stiefvater |  |  |  |  |  |  |  |  |  |
| Vater |  |  |  |  |  |  |  |  |  |

**N**   🔊 Hör gut zu und finde die passenden Bilder.

**O**  **Du bist dran! Wie sind deine Eltern?**

Wir verstehen uns gut/nicht gut, weil _____

_____

_____

_____

Wir streiten uns, weil _____

_____

_____

_____

_____

**P**  **Finde die passenden Wörter und schreib die Sätze richtig auf.**

1 Ich muss        **a** in den Ferien arbeiten.

2 Ich darf nicht      **b** zu Hause helfen.

3 Ich muss um 21 Uhr   **c** nicht in Konzerte gehen.

4 Ich darf keine Freunde  **d** im Bett sein.

5 Ich muss jeden Tag   **e** nach Hause einladen.

6 Ich darf        **f** immer abwaschen.

1  *Ich muss immer abwaschen.*  4 _____

2 _____  5 _____

3 _____  6 _____

**Q**  **Was sagt Sven? Hör gut zu und finde die richtige Reihenfolge für die Bilder.**

a          d

b          e

c          f

**R 1** Schreib Sätze für die Bilder in Übung Q.

a  Ich darf nicht _____ .

b  Ich muss _____ .

c  Ich darf keine _____ .

d  Ich muss _____ .

e  Ich darf nicht _____ .

f  Ich darf keine _____ .

**R 2** 👥 Ist alles richtig? A wählt ein Bild in Übung Q, B antwortet. Dann ist B dran.

*Beispiel:*

A  *Bild a!*

B  *Ich darf nicht ...*

**S** Du bist dran! Was musst du/darfst du nicht zu Hause machen?

_____

_____

_____

_____

_____

| Can you ...? | Listening | Speaking | Reading | Writing |
|---|---|---|---|---|
| say what you look like | | | | |
| ask what someone else looks like | | | | |
| say what someone else looks like | | | | |
| talk about your best friend | | | | |
| describe your own personality | | | | |
| describe someone else's personality | | | | |
| explain why you like your best friend | | | | |
| say how you get on with your best friend | | | | |
| describe your parents | | | | |
| say how you get on with your parents | | | | |
| say why you argue | | | | |
| say what you have to do | | | | |
| say what you're not allowed to do | | | | |

# Mode

**A1** 🔊 **Hör gut zu und sing mit!**

## Ausverkauf

*Junge Mode im Ausverkauf!*
*Junge Mode im Ausverkauf!*

*Ich kaufe dieses T-Shirt*
*Wie gefällt es dir?*
*Es gefällt mir leider nicht*
*Denn es ist viel zu klein!*

### Refrain

*Ich kaufe diese Hose*
*Wie gefällt sie dir?*
*Sie gefällt mir leider nicht*
*Denn sie ist viel zu kurz!*

### Refrain

*Ich kaufe diese Bluse*
*Wie gefällt sie dir?*
*Sie gefällt mir leider nicht*
*Denn sie ist viel zu eng!*

### Refrain

*Ich kaufe diese Mütze*
*Wie gefällt sie dir?*
*Sie gefällt mir leider nicht*
*Denn sie ist viel zu gelb!*

### Refrain

**A2** **Finde die passenden Antworten.**

1 „Ich kaufe diese …" Was heißt
   *diesen/diese/dieses/diese* auf Englisch?

   **a** this/these ☐

   **b** which/what ☐

2 „Wie gefällt es/sie dir?" Was heißt das?

   **a** Was kostet es/sie? ☐

   **b** Wie findest du es/sie? ☐

**A3** **Finde die passenden Bilder für jede Strophe (*verse*).**

a  ☐

b  ☐

c  ☐

d  ☐

**B 1** Was hast du gekauft? Finde elf Plural-Wörter im Worträtsel und schreib sie auf.

_____

_____

_____

**B 2**  Schreib den Singular für die Plural-Wörter auf.

| J | S | D | H | O | S | E | N | D | K | I | R |
|---|---|---|---|---|---|---|---|---|---|---|---|
| E | J | A | C | K | E | N | F | D | T | Y | U |
| A | C | H | E | M | D | E | N | H | S | M | C |
| N | C | N | V | B | J | K | G | D | H | Ü | K |
| S | F | F | D | G | J | P | B | D | I | T | S |
| A | K | P | U | L | L | O | V | E | R | Z | Ä |
| R | Ö | C | K | E | J | P | D | A | T | E | C |
| F | G | B | L | U | S | E | N | G | S | N | K |
| G | E | K | N | B | X | S | C | H | U | H | E |

T-Shirts          T-Shirt

_____          _____

_____          _____

_____          _____

_____          _____

_____          _____

_____          _____

_____          _____

_____          _____

**C** Alexander und seine Cousine Leah sind in der Stadt. Was haben sie gekauft? Hör gut zu und kreuz die passenden Bilder an.

|           |  |  |  |  |  |  |
|-----------|--|--|--|--|--|--|
| Alexander |  |  |  |  |  |  |
| Leah      |  |  |  |  |  |  |

## D1 👥 „Was hast du gekauft?" A deckt Bs Bilder zu und fragt, B antwortet. A schreibt die Antwort auf. Dann ist B dran.

**Beispiel:**

A   *Was hast du gekauft?*

B   *Ich habe zwei Jacken gekauft. Und du?*

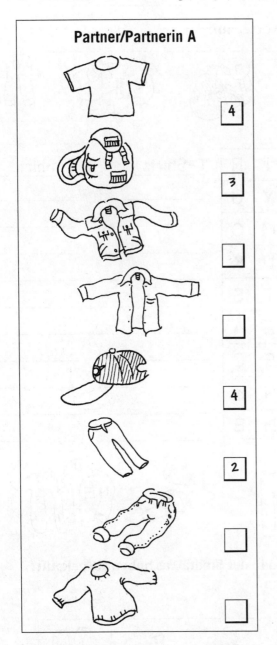
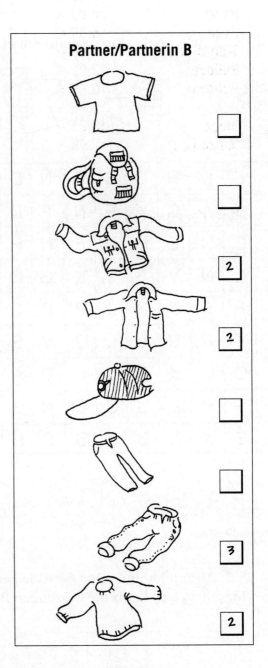

## D2 👥 Was hat dein Partner/deine Partnerin gekauft? Macht Dialoge mit deinen Notizen von Übung D1.

**Beispiel:**

A   *Was habe ich gekauft?*

B   *Du hast vier T-Shirts gekauft, …*

**E**  Du bekommst 100 Euro von deiner Oma und gehst zum Ausverkauf.
Was hast du gekauft? Schreib einen Danke-Brief an deine Oma.

| Junge Mode am Markt | |
| --- | --- |
| Schuhe | 8,99 € |
| Rock | 4,99 € |
| Rock | 5,99 € |
| T-Shirt (x 3) | 9,99 € |
| Pullover | 12,99 € |
| Pullover | 10,99 € |
| Bluse | 10,99 € |
| Bluse | 15,99 € |
| Mütze (x 4) | 15,99 € |

Liebe Oma,
vielen Dank für die 100 Euro! Ich habe viel
gekauft: Ich habe _____
_____
_____
_____
_____
_____

**F**  Finde die passenden Bilder.

1  Diese Jeans gefällt mir sehr gut. ☐

2  Wie gefällt dir dieser Pullover? ☐

3  Dieses Hemd gefällt mir gar nicht! ☐

4  Welche Schuhe gefallen dir? ☐

a

b

c

d

**G** 👥 „Wie gefällt dir … ?" Macht Dialoge mit den Bildern.

*Beispiel:*

**A** *Wie gefällt dir diese Hose?*
**B** *Sie gefällt mir gut.*

**H** **Was sagen sie? Füll die Lücken aus.**

1 Wie gefällt dir dies___ Jacke?

2 Welch___ Hemd gefällt dir?

3 Wie gefällt dir dies___ Rock?

4 Welch___ Jacke gefällt dir?

5 Wie gefällt dir dies___ Kleid?

6 Welch___ Pullover gefällt dir?

**I 1** 📼 Jasmin und Annika kaufen Kleidung. Wie ist alles – was sagt Jasmin?
Hör gut zu und finde die passenden Bilder.

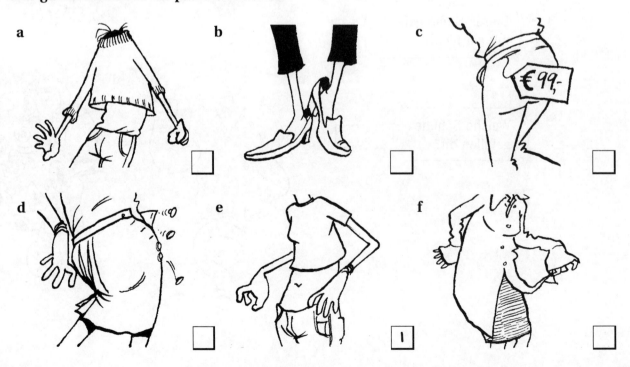

**I2** Schreib dann Sprechblasen für die Bilder.

a

Dieser Pullover ist zu klein!

b

c

d

e

f

**J** Worträtsel: „Was trägst du zur Schule?" Schreib den Satz richtig auf.

eingrünesSweatshirteinengrauenRockeineschwarzeStrumpfhoseundbrauneSchuhe

Ich trage _____

_____ .

**K1**  „Was trägst du zur Schule?" Hör gut zu und schreib die Farben auf.
Male dann die Bilder aus.

1

2

3
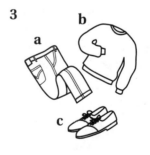

4

a ___grau___

a _____

a _____

a _____

b _____

b _____

b _____

b _____

c _____

c _____

c _____

c _____

**K2** Füll die Lücken aus und finde die passenden Bilder in Übung K1.

1. Ich trage eine blau**e** Jeans und ein grau___ Sweatshirt. Ich trage auch braun___ Schuhe. ☐

3. Ich trage eine gelb___ Bluse. Ich trage einen schwarz___ Rock. Ich trage auch eine blau___ Jacke. ☐

2. Ich trage ein grau___ Hemd und eine rot___ Krawatte. Und ich trage eine schwarz___ Hose. ☐

4. Ich trage ein grün___ Kleid. Ich trage auch einen gelb___ Pullover und ich trage eine rot___ Strumpfhose. ☐

**L** Was trägst du heute zur Schule? A fragt, B beschreibt alles. Dann ist B dran.

*Beispiel:*

**A** *Was trägst du zur Schule?*

**B** *Ich trage ein blaues Sweatshirt, ein …*

**M** Du bist dran! Was trägst du zur Schule?

_____

_____

_____

_____

**N 1** „Was trägst du am liebsten/gern/nicht gern?" Was sagen sie? Hör gut zu und füll die Tabelle aus.

| am liebsten ✔✔ | gern ✔ | nicht gern ✗ |
| --- | --- | --- |

| | | | | | | | | | | | | |
| --- | --- | --- | --- | --- | --- | --- | --- | --- | --- | --- | --- | --- |
| Uwe | | | | | | | | | | | | |
| Heike | | | | | | | | | | | | |
| Martin | | | | | | | | | | | | |
| Steffi | | | | | | | | | | | | |

**N2** 👥 Ratespiel – „Was trägst du am liebsten/gern/nicht gern?" A wählt eine Person von Übung N1 und beschreibt die Kleidung, B rät.

**Beispiel:**

**A**   Ich trage am liebsten Kleider. Ich trage gern Strumpfhosen, aber ich trage nicht gern Turnschuhe.

**B**   Du bist Steffi!

**A**   Ja, richtig!

**O**   Du bist dran! Was trägst du am liebsten/gern/nicht gern?

_____

_____

_____

_____

_____

**P1** Wie findest du deine Uniform? Finde die Adjektive und schreib sie auf.

Meine Uniform ist …

schrecklichhässlichmodernschönunbequemaltmodischpraktischbequemgut

1 _____

2 _____

3 _____

4 _____

5 _____

6 _____

7 _____

8 _____

9 _____

**P2** "Meine Uniform ist …" Macht Dialoge mit den Adjektiven in Übung P1.

*Beispiel:*

**A** *Wie findest du deine Uniform?*

**B** *Meine Uniform ist schrecklich.*

**Q1** Finde die passenden Sätze für die Bilder.

a

b

c

d

**1** Meine Uniform ist gut, weil sie praktisch ist.

**2** Ich finde meine Uniform schlecht, weil sie unbequem ist.

**3** Ich finde meine Uniform gut, weil sie modern ist.

**4** Meine Uniform ist hässlich, weil sie altmodisch ist.

**Q2** Eine Austauschklasse in Deutschland fragt: „Wie findest du deine Uniform?" Schreib Sätze
für diese Schüler/Schülerinnen mit „Meine Uniform ist gut/schlecht, weil …"

hässlich: Meine Uniform ist schlecht, weil sie hässlich ist.

bequem: _____

schrecklich: _____

schön: _____

**R** Du bist dran! Zeichne deine Traumuniform! Was trägst du? Schreib die Wörter auf.
Wie findest du deine Uniform? Schreib zwei Sätze.

Ich trage _____

_____

_____

Ich finde meine Uniform _____

_____

_____

| Can you …? | Listening | Speaking | Reading | Writing |
| --- | --- | --- | --- | --- |
| ask others what clothes they have bought | | | | |
| say what clothes you have bought | | | | |
| ask others their opinion on items of clothing | | | | |
| give your opinion on items of clothing | | | | |
| ask others what they wear to school | | | | |
| say what you wear for school | | | | |
| state what colours certain clothes are | | | | |
| ask others what clothes they like wearing | | | | |
| say what clothes you like wearing | | | | |
| ask and say what your favourite clothes are | | | | |
| ask for and give opinions on school uniform | | | | |

# 5 Wie war die Party?

## A1 🔊 Hör gut zu und sing mit!

### Party-Rap

*Mein Geburtstag ist heute*
*Am 8. April!*
*Und ich mache eine Party*
*Hurra!*
*Kommst du?*
*Ja, ja, gern!*

*Wo ist die Party?*
*Im Partykeller!*
*Wie ist die Adresse?*
*Goldstraße 13!*
*Wann ist die Party?*
*Um 18 Uhr!*

*Herzlichen Glückwunsch!*
*Danke – vielen Dank!*
*Was hast du bekommen?*
*Einen Fußball*
*Einen Gutschein*
*Ein Rad und ein Buch*

*Wie war die Party?*
*Super – super und toll!*
*Was hast du gemacht?*
*Mit Tina getanzt*
*Pizza gegessen*
*und Cola getrunken*

## A2 Finde die passenden Antworten.

1 Was gibt es am 8. April?

  a Eine Geburtstagsparty. ☐

  b Ein Picknick im Park. ☐

2 „Der Partykeller" – was ist das?

  a Ein Zimmer für Feste und Partys. ☐

  b Eine Garage für Fahrräder und Autos. ☐

3 Deine Freundin hat Geburtstag. Was sagst du?

  a Frohe Weihnachten! ☐

  b Herzlichen Glückwunsch! ☐

## B Finde die passenden Bilder für jede Strophe (verse).

a        b

☐        ☐

c        d

☐        ☐

**C** **Wann haben sie Geburtstag? Füll die Lücken aus.**

1

März

2
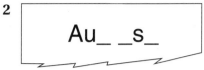
Au_ _s_

3

J_l_

4
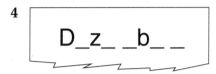
D_z_ _b_ _

5
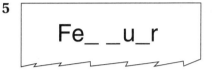
Fe_ _u_r

6
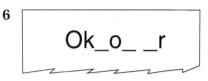
Ok_o_ _r

7

A_r_ _

8
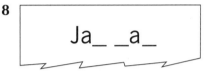
Ja_ _a_

9
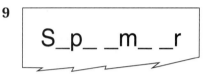
S_p_ _m_ _r

10

M_ _

11
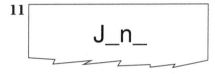
J_n_

12
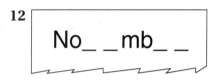
No_ _mb_ _

**D** 🔊 **Familie Mai hat im Mai Geburtstag! Hör gut zu und finde die passenden Zahlen.**

| Mai | | | | | | |
|---|---|---|---|---|---|---|
| 1 | 2 | 3 | 4 | 5 | 6 | 7 |
| 8 | 9 | 10 | 11 | 12 | 13 | 14 |
| 15 | 16 | 17 | 18 | 19 | 20 | 21 |
| 22 | 23 | 24 | 25 | 26 | 27 | (28) |
| 29 | 30 | 31 | | | | |

**E 1** 🔊 **Wann haben Majas Freundinnen und Freunde Geburtstag? Sie schreibt ihr Tagebuch – aber sie macht Fehler. Hör gut zu und korrigiere die Fehler.**

| | | |
|---|---|---|
| Suse | 3. August | |
| Simon | ²⁹. 9̶. April | 29. April |
| Annika | 24. Juni | |
| Michael | 21. November | |
| Hanna | 8. Januar | |
| Ralf | 31. Juli | |
| Kathi | 27. Mai | |
| Daniel | 26. September | |

**E2** 👥👥 **Ist alles richtig? A fragt, B antwortet. Dann ist B dran.**

*Beispiel:*

A *Wann hat Suse Geburtstag?*

B *Sie hat am 3. August Geburtstag.*

**F** 👥👥 **Wann hast du Geburtstag? Macht Dialoge mit den Bildern.**

**G** **Du bist dran! Wann hast du Geburtstag? Wann hat deine Familie Geburtstag? Wann haben deine Freunde/Freundinnen Geburtstag?**

_____

_____

_____

_____

_____

**H** **Was ist das? Finde die passenden Bilder.**

**1** Heiligabend ☐   **2** Ostern ☐   **3** Nikolaustag ☐   **4** Diwali ☐

**5** Silvester ☐   **6** Id-ul-Fitr (Ende Ramadan) ☐   **7** Fasching/Karneval ☐

**I** Sieh auch Lehrbuch, Seite 61, Übung 5a. Wann sind diese Feiertage? Lies die Sätze.
Richtig oder falsch? Schreib ✔ oder ✗ und korrigiere dann die falschen Sätze.

| | Richtig/Falsch? | Richtige Sätze |
|---|---|---|
| **1** Heiligabend ist am 25. Dezember. | | |
| **2** Ostern ist im März/April. | | |
| **3** Nikolaustag ist am 16. Dezember. | | |
| **4** Diwali ist am 7. November. | | |
| **5** Silvester ist am 1. Januar. | | |
| **6** Id-ul-Fitr ist im Januar/Februar. | | |
| **7** Fasching/Karneval ist im September. | | |

**J** Finde die passenden Bilder.

**1** Wir machen am Montag eine Faschingsfete. ☐

**2** Ich habe am Samstag Geburtstag. Ich mache eine Party. ☐

**3** Meine Schule macht am Freitag ein Schulfest. ☐

**4** Wir machen am Sonntag ein Picknick. ☐

a   b

c   d

**K** 🔊 Luise macht eine Party und schreibt eine Einladung.
Hör gut zu und füll die Lücken aus.

**Einladung – Einladung – Einladung**

zur _____

Ich habe am _____ Geburtstag und

mache um _____ Uhr eine Fete!

Wo: im _____

Adresse: _____

**L** Du bist dran! Schreib eine Einladung. Zeichne auch passende Bilder für die Party auf die Einladung.

Einladung

**M1** Wo ist die Party? Schreib die Wörter richtig auf. Füll dann die Lücken rechts aus.

a ZIMWOMERHN **im Wohnzimmer**

b CISOD _____

c KELRAPLERYT _____

d KPRA _____

e MIDABHMCSW _____

f LUSCHE _____

**M2** Ist alles richtig? Macht Dialoge.

*Beispiel:*

A *Bild a! Ich mache eine Party. Kommst du?*

B *Ja, gern. Wo ist die Party?*

A *Im Wohnzimmer.*

## N 1 Diese Freunde und Freundinnen kommen nicht zu Atalays Party. Was sagen sie? Finde die passenden Bilder.

**Ich kann leider nicht kommen!**

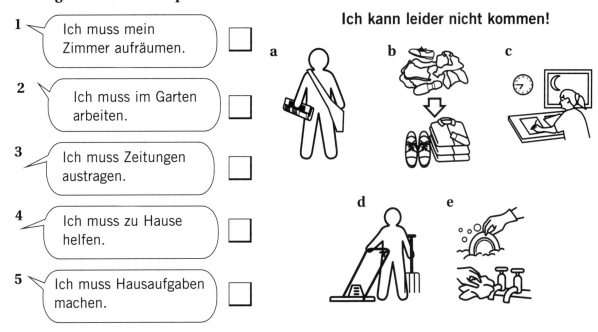

1 Ich muss mein Zimmer aufräumen. ☐

2 Ich muss im Garten arbeiten. ☐

3 Ich muss Zeitungen austragen. ☐

4 Ich muss zu Hause helfen. ☐

5 Ich muss Hausaufgaben machen. ☐

## N2 Was sagst du? A wählt ein Bild von Übung N1, B antwortet. Dann ist B dran.

*Beispiel:*

**A**  *Bild a!*

**B**  *Ich kann leider nicht kommen. Ich muss Zeitungen austragen.*

## O Tom muss aufräumen. Wo ist … ? Finde 8 Wörter und schreib sie auf. Schreib auch den passenden Artikel (*der, die, das*) auf.

```
L W D Y W Ü R S T C H E N Q X O D
K D S C D S P I E L E R S V K A C
H J R L U F T B A L L O N S X Z Q
G K A R T O F F E L S A L A T M B
P V K A P F E L S A F T Y C D S Z
K A S S E T T E N R E C O R D E R
J Q C O L I M O N A D E P L D V Y
```

1 _____

2 _____

3 _die Würstchen_

4 _____

5 _____

6 _____

7 _____

8 _____

**P** 🔊 **Wo ist alles? Hör gut zu und finde die passenden Bilder.**

a ☐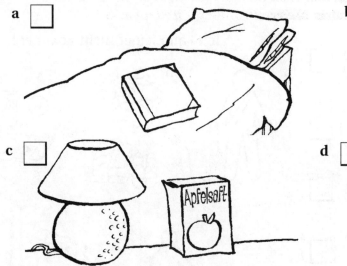

b ☐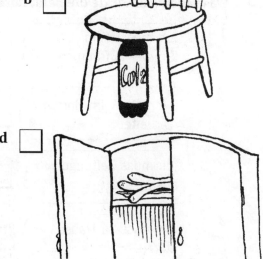

c ☐

d ☐

**Q** **Füll die Lücken aus.**

1 Die Würstchen sind _____ dem Schreibtisch.

2 Der _____ ist unter dem Stuhl.

3 Die Luftballons sind in dem _____ .

4 Der Kartoffelsalat ist _____ dem Stuhl.

5 Der _____ ist auf dem Computer.

6 Der Kassettenrecorder ist im _____ .

7 Die CDs sind _____ dem _____ .

8 Die _____ ist _____ dem Regal.

**R** **Wo ist alles? Füll die Lücken mit *dem* oder *der* aus.**

1 Die CDs sind in d____ Kleiderschrank.

2 Der Kartoffelsalat ist neben d____ Computer.

3 Die Luftballons sind auf d____ Regal.

4 Die Würstchen sind unter d____ Stuhl.

5 Der Kassettenrecorder ist neben d____ Stuhl.

6 Der Apfelsaft ist auf d____ Schreibtisch.

**S** 👥 **Dein Partner/Deine Partnerin muss aufräumen – und du auch!**
**Wo ist alles? Macht Dialoge.**

*Beispiel:*

A   *Wo sind die Würstchen?*

B   *Die Würstchen sind auf dem Bett.*

**T1**   **Was hast du zum Geburtstag bekommen? Schreib die passenden Wörter auf.**

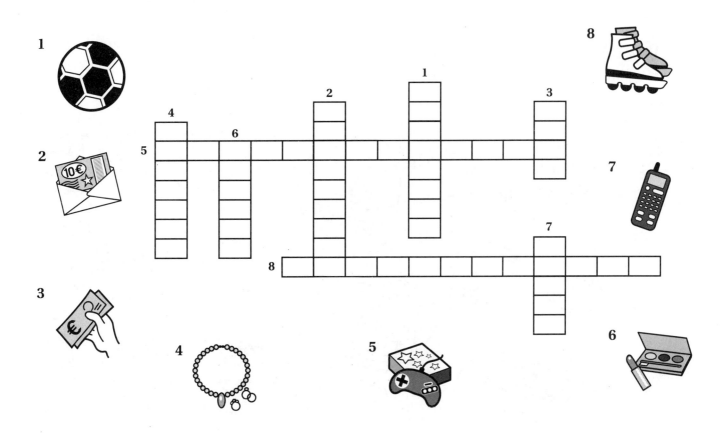

**T2** 👥 **Ist alles richtig? Was hast du zum Geburtstag bekommen?**
**Macht Dialoge mit den Bildern in Übung T1.**

*Beispiel:*

**A**   *Was hast du zum Geburtstag bekommen?*

**B**   *Ich habe einen Gutschein bekommen.*

**U**   📼 **Was haben Miriam und Thorsten zum Geburtstag bekommen?**
**Hör gut zu und kreuz die passenden Bilder an.**

| | | | | | | | | |
|---|---|---|---|---|---|---|---|---|
| Miriam | | | | | | | | |
| Thorsten | | | | | | | | |

**V**   **Finde die passenden Wörter.**

1  Ich habe Cola                      **a**  gespielt.

2  Ich habe mit Anna          **b**  getroffen.

3  Wir haben Pizza            **c**  getrunken.

4  Ich habe Gitarre           **d**  getanzt.

5  Ich habe Lars und Ute     **e**  gegessen.

**W**   👥 **Wie war deine Party – was hast du bekommen und gemacht?**
**Macht Dialoge mit den Bildern.**

*Beispiel:*

**A**   *Wie war deine Party?*

**B**   *Super!*

**A**   *Was hast du gemacht?*

**B**   *Ich habe Gitarre gespielt.*

**X 1 Lies Lolas Brief und füll die Lücken aus.**

Hallo Sarah!

Meine _____ am Samstag war super! Ich habe viele

Geschenke _____ und wir haben viel _____ : Wir

haben _____ getrunken und Kartoffelsalat _____

- lecker! Ich habe auch _____ gespielt und ich habe

mit Martin _____ ! Ich habe auch Marias Cousine

_____ getroffen - sie ist sehr nett. Aber jetzt muss

ich leider den Partykeller aufräumen …

Tschüs!

Lola

| |
|---|
| getanzt |
| Apfelsaft |
| Geburtstagsparty |
| gegessen |
| Monika |
| bekommen |
| Gitarre |
| gemacht |

**X2 Du bist dran! Schreib einen Brief so wie Lola mit den Informationen unten.**

_____

_____

_____

_____

| Can you …? | Listening | Speaking | Reading | Writing |
|---|---|---|---|---|
| say when your birthday is | | | | |
| ask and say when special events/celebrations are | | | | |
| invite others to a party | | | | |
| accept invitations | | | | |
| make excuses | | | | |
| ask where things are | | | | |
| describe where things are | | | | |
| ask others what birthday presents they received | | | | |
| say what birthday presents you received | | | | |
| ask and give your opinion about parties or events | | | | |

# Wir gehen in die Stadt

**A** Was kann man in der Stadt machen? Finde die Gebäude und schreib sie auf.

1 DELESIEI __EISDIELE__

2 OFSDTFOA-SRETATURNA _____

3 SMBCHIMWAD _____

4 HNSIAEB _____

5 ZTZUMFREETINIER _____

6 EJUNMZEGNTRUD _____

7 OKNI _____

8 FÉAC _____

9 MSUMEU _____

10 ATHRETE _____

**B1** Was kann man in Basel machen? Hör gut zu und finde die richtige Reihenfolge für die Bilder.

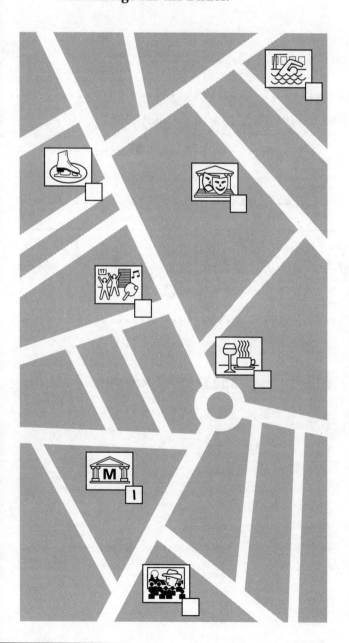

**B2** Was kann man in Basel machen? Macht Dialoge mit den Bildern in Übung B1.

*Beispiel:*

**A** *Was kann man in Basel machen?*

**B** *Man kann ins Museum gehen.*

**B3** Du bist dran! Was kann man in deiner Stadt machen?

_____

_____

_____

_____

_____

_____

_____

_____

_____

_____

**C** Lies Gabis E-Mail und die Sätze. Sind sie richtig oder falsch? Schreib ✔ oder ✗.

Hallo Gisela!

Wo willst du am Freitag zu Mittag essen? Wir können ein Picknick machen oder wir können ins Café oder ins Fastfood-Restaurant gehen. Wohin willst du gehen? Ich will im Fastfood-Restaurant essen – ich esse sehr gern Fastfood!

Am Nachmittag können wir in die Eisbahn oder ins Hallenbad gehen. Mein Bruder will ins Museum gehen, aber das finde ich sehr langweilig. Ich will auch einen Einkaufsbummel machen. Und du?

Bis bald!

Gabi

|   |   | Richtig/Falsch? |
|---|---|---|
| 1 | Gabi will am Freitag ein Picknick machen. | |
| 2 | Gabi will im Park essen. | |
| 3 | Gabi mag Fastfood nicht. | |
| 4 | Gabi will am Nachmittag in die Eisdiele gehen. | |
| 5 | Sie will auch mit ihrem Bruder ins Museum gehen. | |
| 6 | Gabi will einkaufen gehen. | |

**D 1 Füll die Lücken aus.**

1 Man __kann__ ins Kino gehen.

2 Wir _____ einen Einkaufsbummel machen.

3 Ich _____ in die Eisdiele gehen.

4 _____ du ein Picknick machen?

5 Ich _____ in die Disco gehen.

6 Man _____ ins Jugendzentrum gehen.

| kann | Willst | will | kann | will | können |
|---|---|---|---|---|---|

**D 2 Was will Familie Haab heute machen?**
**Füll die Sprechblasen aus.**

1  Ich will ins Fastfood-Restaurant und in die Eisbahn gehen.

2

3

4

5

**E** Du bist dran! Was willst du am Wochenende machen?

Ich will _____

_____

_____

_____

**F** „Wo treffen wir uns?" Füll die Lücken aus.

| | | |
|---|---|---|
| **a** _____ Busbahnhof. | | an der |
| **b** _____ Eisdiele. | | vor der |
| **c** _____ Bahnhof. | | vor dem |
| **d** _____ Imbissstube. | | in der |
| **e** _____ Markt. | | im |
| **f** _____ Bushaltestelle. | | am |
| **g** _____ Eisbahn. | | in der |
| **h** _____ Café. | | am |

**G** „Wo treffen wir uns?" Schreib Sätze.

**a** vor    Wir treffen uns vor dem Café. _____

**b** an    _____

**c** vor   _____

**d** an    _____

**e** an    _____

**f** vor   _____

## H 1 ▱ Wohin gehen sie oder wo sind sie? Hör gut zu und finde die passenden Bilder.

1 a ✔  b ☐

4 a 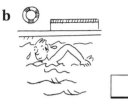 Schwimmbad ☐  b ☐

2 a  SUPERMARKT ☐  b ☐

5 a Freizeitzentrum ☐  b  ☐

3 a  Eisdiele ☐  b  ☐

## H 2 *in* + Akkusativ oder Dativ? Ergänze die Sätze für die anderen Bilder in Übung H1.

1 Gabi und ich sind _____ Park.

2 Ich gehe heute _____ Supermarkt.

3 Ich gehe mit Susi _____ Eisdiele.

4 Ich bin _____ Schwimmbad.

5 Ich gehe morgens _____ Freizeitzentrum.

## I „Wohin gehen wir? Wo treffen wir uns?" Macht Dialoge mit den Informationen unten.

**Beispiel:**

A  *Wohin gehen wir heute Abend?*

B  *Gehen wir in die Disco?*

A  *Ja, okay. Und wo treffen wir uns?*

B  *Treffen wir uns im Café?*

A  *Okay!*

| Gehen wir in … ? | Treffen wir uns in … ? |
|---|---|
| a | a |
| b | b DB |
| c | c |
| d | d |
| e | e |

**Du bist dran! Wohin gehst du am Wochenende? Wo triffst du deinen Freund/deine Freundin?**

_____

_____

_____

_____

**K**  Was ist das? Schreib die Wörter auf.

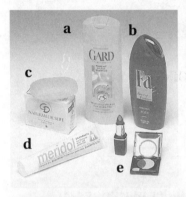
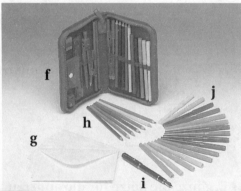
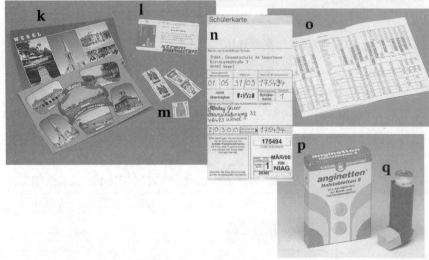

a _____Shampoo_____

b _____

c _____

d _____

e _____

f _____

g _____

h _____

i _____

j _____

k _____

l _____

m _____

n _____

o _____

p _____

q _____

**L1**  Finde die passenden Wörter für die Geschäfte.

die Post      der Busbahnhof
der Schreibwarenladen      die Apotheke
die Drogerie

a  _____

b  _____

c  _____

d  _____

e  _____

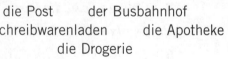

**L2** Wohin musst du gehen? Schreib Sprechblasen für die Bilder in Übung L1.

1 Ich muss zur Apotheke gehen.

2

3

4

5

**M1** 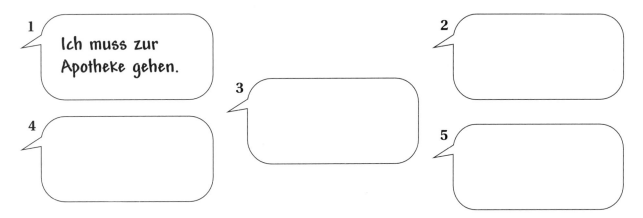 Was brauchen sie? Hör gut zu und kreuz die passenden Bilder an.

| | | | Monatskarte | | | | | Duschgel | | | ZAHNPASTA |
|---|---|---|---|---|---|---|---|---|---|---|---|
| Kris | | | | | | | | | | | |
| Gabi | | | | | | | | | | | |
| Anke | | | | | | | | | | | |
| Peter | | | | | | | | | | | |
| Britta | | | | | | | | | | | |

**M2** Was brauchen sie? Macht Dialoge mit den Informationen in Übung M1.

*Beispiel:*

**A** *Was brauchst du, Kris?*

**B** *Ich brauche einen Füller und eine Federmappe.*

**M3** Schreib dann Sätze mit *keinen/keine/kein/keine*.

Kris:   Ich habe keinen Füller und keine Federmappe.

Gabi: _____

Anke: _____

Peter: _____

Britta: _____

**N** 👥 **Labyrinth-Spiel: A wählt einen Buchstaben, B beschreibt, was er/sie braucht; A sagt, wohin B gehen muss.**

*Beispiel:*

**A** *Du bist D!*

**B** *Ich brauche Shampoo und ich habe keine Seife und kein Make-up!*

**A** *Du musst zur Drogerie gehen!*

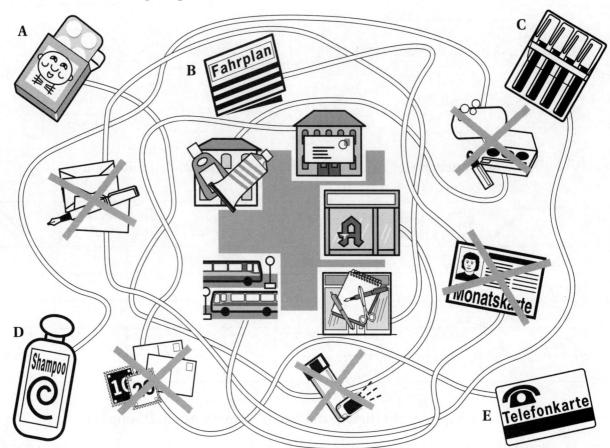

**O** **Was gibt es im Fundbüro? Schreib die Wörter auf. Schreib auch *der*, *die* oder *das* auf.**

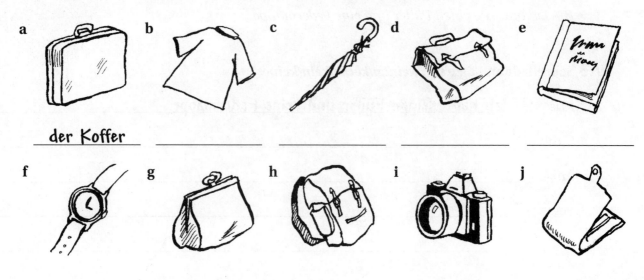

a    der Koffer

b    _____

c    _____

d    _____

e    _____

f    _____

g    _____

h    _____

i    _____

j    _____

**P**  Lies die Sätze und finde die passenden Wörter.

1  Ich habe (meine) /meinen Tasche verloren.

2  Ich habe mein / meine Buch verloren.

3  Ich habe mein / meinen Schirm verloren.

4  Ich habe meine / mein Uhr verloren.

5  Ich habe meine / meinen Koffer verloren.

6  Ich habe meinen / mein Rucksack verloren.

**Q1**  Was haben Niki und Gerd verloren? Füll die Lücken aus.

Niki

Ich habe _____ Tasche, _____ Geldbörse, _____ Buch und _____ Uhr verloren.

Gerd

Ich habe _____ Rucksack, _____ T-Shirt, _____ Schirm und _____ Brieftasche verloren.

**Q2**  🔊 Ist alles richtig? Hör gut zu.

**R1**  Wie ist er/sie/es? Finde die passenden Bilder.

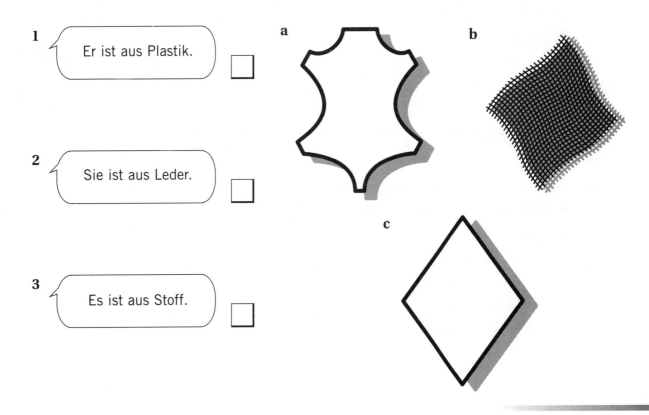

1  Er ist aus Plastik. ☐

2  Sie ist aus Leder. ☐

3  Es ist aus Stoff. ☐

a

b

c

**R2** *Er, sie* oder *es?* Füll die Lücken aus.

1 Ich habe meine Geldbörse verloren. __Sie__ ist grün und aus Leder.

2 Mein T-Shirt ist blau und weiß. _____ ist ganz neu.

3 Meine Tasche ist ganz groß und _____ ist aus Stoff.

4 Wo ist mein T-Shirt?! _____ war hier auf dem Stuhl!

5 Und mein Pullover! Wo ist _____?

6 Haben Sie mein Buch? _____ ist ein großes Schulbuch.

**S1** 🔊 Wie sieht er/sie/es aus? Hör gut zu und füll die Tabelle aus.

| | Farbe(n) | | | |
|---|---|---|---|---|
| | braun, schwarz | ✔ | | |
| | | | | |
| | | | | |
| | | | | |
| | | | | |
| | | | | |

**S2** 👥 Was hast du verloren? A ist Beamter/Beamtin, B hat etwas verloren. Macht Dialoge mit den Informationen in Übung S1.

*Beispiel:*

**A** *Guten Tag! Kann ich Ihnen helfen?*

**B** *Ja, bitte. Ich habe meine Geldbörse verloren.*

**A** *Wie sieht sie aus?*

**B** *Sie ist braun und schwarz. Sie ist aus Leder.*

**T**   Was hast du verloren? Male die Bilder aus und schreib eine Karte.

*Beispiel:*

> VERLOREN!
>
> Mein Rucksack!
>
> Ich habe meinen Rucksack verloren!
>
> Er ist rot und aus Leder und er ist sehr alt.
>
> Frau M. Braun
>
> Telefon 0112 787 653

| Can you …? | Listening | Speaking | Reading | Writing |
|---|---|---|---|---|
| ask and say what there is to do in a town | | | | |
| say what you want to do | | | | |
| ask and say where you plan to meet | | | | |
| describe what you do not have | | | | |
| describe what you need | | | | |
| say where you need to go for these things | | | | |
| ask if you can help someone | | | | |
| describe what you have lost | | | | |
| ask and describe what it looks like | | | | |
| express concern about the loss | | | | |

# Meine Umgebung

## A1 🔊 Hör gut zu und sing mit!

### Stadt und Land

| 1 | Busse und Gebäude |
|---|---|
| 2 | Lärm und viele Leute |
| 3 | Straßenbahnen, Motorräder |
| 4 | Altpapier und Müll |
| | |
| 5 | Blumen, Tiere, Bäume |
| 6 | Lämmer in der Scheune |
| 7 | Schmetterlinge, Seen, Wälder |
| 8 | Erde, Wasser, Luft |

## A2 Finde die passenden Bilder für jede Wortreihe.

a  ☐

b  ☐

c  ☐

d  ☐

e  ☐

f  ☐

g  ☐

h  ☐

**B 1** Was gibt es in deiner Stadt? Schreib die Wörter richtig auf.

1 NEUSKKNAHAR _____

2 SASPSERKA _____

3 TOLEH _____

4 DIFULALßABNOTS _____

5 SCHTEGEÄF _____

6 OZO _____

7 DUBEGEÄ _____

8 ZENNIEMURTSUFAK _____

9 LENATSKELT _____

10 RKPA _____

**B 2** Finde die passenden Bilder für die Wörter in Übung B1.

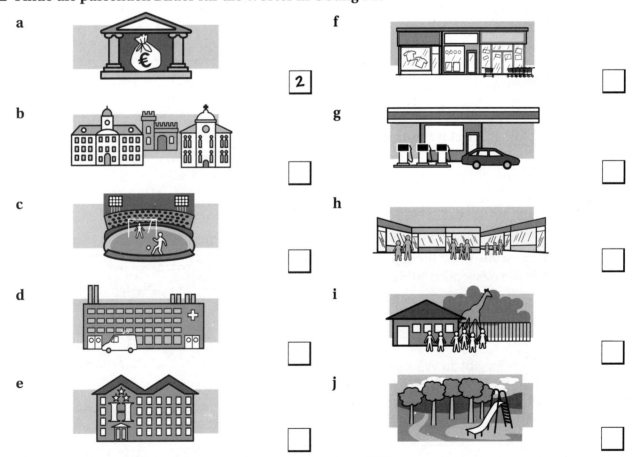

a ☐ 2

b ☐

c ☐

d ☐

e ☐

f ☐

g ☐

h ☐

i ☐

j ☐

**B 3** 📼 Was gibt es alles in Münster? Hör gut zu und finde die richtige Reihenfolge für die Bilder in Übung B2.

_c, ..._ _____

**B 4** 👥 Was gibt es in Münster? A fragt und zeigt auf ein Bild von Übung B2, B antwortet. Dann ist B dran.
*Beispiel:*
*A* *Was gibt es in Münster? (Bild a)*
*B* *Es gibt eine Sparkasse.*

## C1 🔊 Potsdam ist eine tolle Stadt! Was gibt es dort – und wie ist alles? Hör gut zu und kreuz die passenden Wörter an.

| | alt | groß | klein | modern | neu | interessant | schön |
|---|---|---|---|---|---|---|---|
| 🏰 | | | | | | | |
| 🏛 | | | | | | | |
| 🏟 | | | | | | | |
| 🏬 | | | | | | | |
| 🏠 | | | | | | | |
| 🏫 | | | | | | | |
| 🌳 | | | | | | | |

## C2 👥 Ist alles richtig? A fragt B, antwortet.

*Beispiel:*

A  *Was gibt es in Potsdam?*

B  *Es gibt ein kleines Einkaufszentrum.*

## D Warum wohnt Tim nicht gern in Potsdam? Finde die passenden Bilder.

1 Es gibt zu viele Autos. ☐

2 Es gibt zu viel Lärm. ☐

3 Es gibt keine Natur. ☐

4 Es gibt zu viel Verkehr. ☐

5 Es gibt zu viel Umweltverschmutzung. ☐

a

b

c

d

e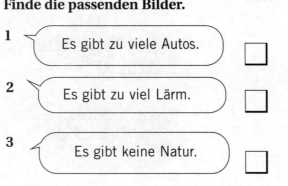

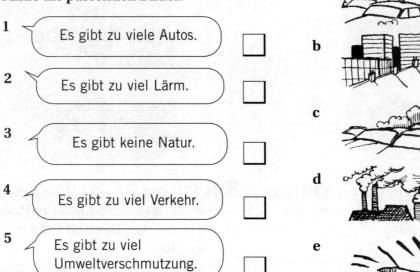

**E** 🔊 **Warum wohnen Daniel und Kathi nicht gern in Rostock?**
**Hör gut zu und füll die Tabelle aus.**

|  |  |  |  |  |  |
|---|---|---|---|---|---|
| Daniel |  |  |  |  |  |
| Kathi |  |  |  |  |  |

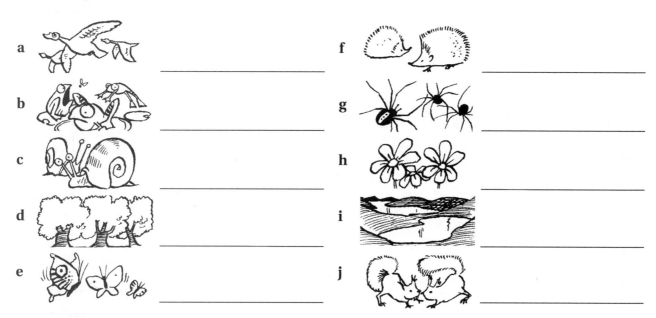

**F** **Du bist dran! Wohnst du gern/nicht gern in der Stadt? Warum (nicht)?**

_____

_____

_____

_____

**G1** **Was gibt es auf dem Land? Schreib die Wörter auf.**

a _____

b _____

c _____

d _____

e _____

f _____

g _____

h _____

i _____

j _____

**G2** 👥 **Ist alles richtig? A wählt ein Bild, B antwortet. Dann ist B dran.**

_Beispiel:_

A  _Was gibt es auf dem Land? Bild a!_

B  _Es gibt Vögel._

A  _Richtig!_

**G3** 👥👥 **Warum wohnst du gern auf dem Land? A fragt, B wählt ein Bild und antwortet mit *Ich wohne gern hier, weil es … gibt*. Dann ist B dran.**

*Beispiel:*

**A** *Warum wohnst du gern auf dem Land?*

**B** *Ich wohne gern hier, weil es Vögel gibt.*

**H** 📼 „Ich wohne gern/nicht gern auf dem Land, weil …" Wer sagt was? Hör gut zu und schreib *E* (Erdal) oder *A* (Anna) auf.

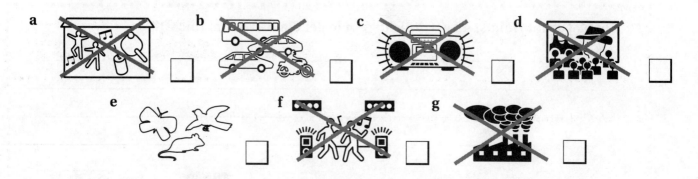

**I1** **Lies Inas Brief und die Sätze. Sind sie richtig oder falsch?**

| | | Richtig | Falsch |
|---|---|---|---|
| Meine Familie und ich – wir wohnen in einem Dorf. Ich wohne gern auf dem Land. Es gibt keinen Verkehr – das finde ich gut. Aber ich wohne auch nicht gern hier, weil es langweilig ist! Meine Schwester – sie ist 6 Jahre alt – wohnt gern hier, weil es viele Tiere gibt. Und ich wohne gern auf dem Land, weil es keinen Lärm gibt. Das finde ich gut. Aber für die Jugend gibt es hier nicht viel: Es gibt zum Beispiel keine Disco! Aber ich wohne gern auf dem Land, weil es hier keine Umweltverschmutzung gibt – das finde ich wichtig. | **1** Es gibt viele Autos. | | |
| | **2** Es gibt nichts zu tun. | | |
| | **3** Es gibt viel Natur. | | |
| | **4** Sie wohnt gern hier, weil es sehr ruhig ist. | | |
| | **5** Sie wohnt gern hier, weil es auch eine Disco gibt. | | |
| | **6** Es gibt zu viel Umweltverschmutzung. | | |

**I2** Du bist dran! Warum wohnst du gern/nicht gern auf dem Land?
Schreib einen Brief so wie Ina mit den Informationen unten.

_____

_____

_____

_____

_____

**J1** Was ist Umwelt? Finde die passenden Wörter für die Bilder.

1 Menschen

2 Wasser

3 Luft

4 Verkehr

5 Fabriken

6 Müll

7 Wald

8 Erde

9 Pflanzen

10 Kraftwerke

11 Zigaretten

12 Pestizide

13 Lärm

14 Tiere

**J2** Ratespiel: A wählt ein Wort und buchstabiert es, B rät das Wort.
Dann ist B dran.

_Beispiel:_

_A_ M –

_B_ Müll!

_A_ Nein! M – E –

_B_ Menschen!

_A_ Richtig!

**K** 🅦📖 Lies die Wörter in Übung J1. Welche Wörter sind im Plural – und welche sind im Singular? Schreib zwei Listen.

| Singular | Plural |
|----------|--------|
| Wasser | Menschen |

**L** 🅦📖 Finde den Singular für die Plural-Wörter in Übung K. Schau im Wörterbuch nach und schreib sie auf.

| Plural | Singular |
|--------|----------|
| Menschen | Mensch |

**M1** Welche Wörter sind was? Ordne sie unter die passenden Überschriften.

Vögel    Blumen    Coladosen    Kinder    Verkehr
Papier    Chipstüten         Erwachsene
Pferde    Jugendliche    Seen    Mineralwasser    Autos    Gemüse
Schwimmbad    Frösche    Bäume    Kassettenrecorder

| Lärm | Menschen | Müll | Pflanzen | Tiere | Wasser |
|------|----------|------|----------|-------|--------|
|  |  |  |  |  |  |

**M2** 👥 **Ist alles richtig? A fragt, B antwortet. Dann ist B dran.**

*Beispiel:*

**A** *Was ist Lärm?*

**B** *Autos, …*

**N** 📼 **Was ist das größte Problem für die Umwelt – was sagen Uwe, Klara, Heiko und Vanessa? Hör gut zu und finde die passenden Bilder für jede Person.**

a  _____

c  _____

b  _____ Uwe _____

d  _____

**O** **Was sagen sie? Füll die Lücken aus.**

1 Lärm ist schlimm. Aber Verkehr ist schlimm_____ als Lärm. Und Fabriken sind am schlimm_____ !

2 Zigaretten sind gefährlich. Und Pestizide sind gefährlich_____ _____ Zigaretten. Aber Kraftwerke sind _____ _____ !

3 Müll ist umweltfeindlich. Aber Fabriken sind _____ _____ Müll. Und Pestizide sind _____ _____ !

**P1** „Ich bin umweltfreundlich!" **Finde die passenden Bilder.**

a  b

c

d  e

1 Ich fahre mit dem Rad. ☐

2 Ich bringe Flaschen zum Altglascontainer. ☐

3 Ich trenne meinen Müll. ☐

4 Ich bringe Altpapier zum Altpapiercontainer. ☐

5 Ich kaufe Recyclingpapier. ☐

**P2** Das ist nicht umweltfreundlich! Finde die passenden Wörter und schreib die Sätze richtig auf.

1 Ich nehme     a in Dosen.     _____

2 Ich fahre     b Plastiktüten.     _____

3 Ich trenne     c jeden Tag.     _____

4 Ich bade     d mit dem Auto.     _____

5 Ich kaufe Cola     e meinen Müll nicht.     _____

**P3** 👥 Wie bist du? A sagt: „Du bist umweltfreundlich/umweltfeindlich", B wählt einen Satz und antwortet. Dann ist B dran.

*Beispiel:*

**A** *Du bist umweltfreundlich! Was machst du?*

**B** *Ich trenne meinen Müll.*

**Q1** Müll in der Schule – was ist das alles? Finde die passenden Wörter.

1 eine Chipstüte ☐

2 eine Postkarte ☐

3 ein halbes Brötchen ☐

4 eine Flasche Apfelsaft ☐

5 ein Buch ☐

6 eine Coladose ☐

7 ein Glas Jogurt ☐

8 eine Jugendzeitschrift ☐

9 eine Mineralwasserflasche ☐

10 ein altes Schulheft ☐

a
b
c
d
e
f
g
h
i
j

**Q2** Was kommt wohin? Schreib die Wörter von Übung Q1 in die passenden Container.

### Altpapiercontainer

### Müll

### Altglascontainer

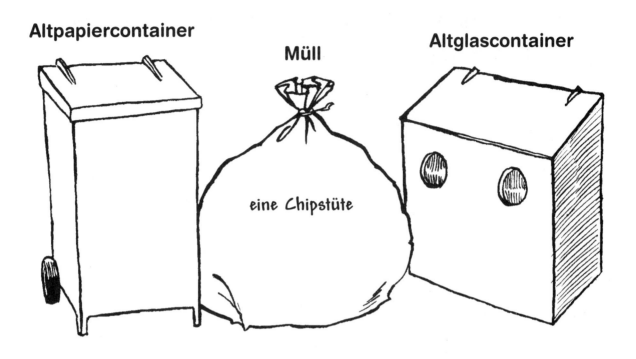

eine Chipstüte

**Q3** [🔊] Ist alles richtig? Hör gut zu.

**R** Du bist dran! Was machst du für die Umwelt?

_____

_____

_____

_____

| Can you ...? | Listening | Speaking | Reading | Writing |
|---|---|---|---|---|
| describe your town | | | | |
| give your opinion about living in a town | | | | |
| describe the country | | | | |
| give your opinion about living in the country | | | | |
| identify names and items linked to the environment | | | | |
| talk about the most serious problems for the environment | | | | |
| talk about actions that help or damage the environment | | | | |

# 8 Gesundes Leben

## A1 🔊 Hör gut zu und sing mit!

### Au, au, au!

*Wo tut es weh?*
*Wo tut es weh?*
*Was fehlt dir?*
*Wo tut es weh?*

1   *Mein Arm tut weh!*
    *Au, au, au!*

    ***Refrain***

2   *Mein Bein tut weh!*
    *Mein Arm tut weh!*
    *Au, au, au!*

    ***Refrain***

3   *Mein Knie tut weh!*
    *Mein Bein tut weh!*
    *Mein Arm tut weh!*
    *Au, au, au!*

    ***Refrain***

4   *Mein Fuß tut weh!*
    *Mein Knie tut weh!*
    *Mein Bein tut weh!*
    *Mein Arm tut weh!*
    *Au, au, au!*

    ***Refrain***

5   *Mein Kopf tut weh!*
    *Mein Fuß tut weh!*
    *Mein Knie tut weh!*
    *Mein Bein tut weh!*
    *Mein Arm tut weh!*
    *Au, au, au!*

    ***Refrain***

## A2 📖 Wo tut es weh? Finde die passenden Bilder für die Sätze 1–5.

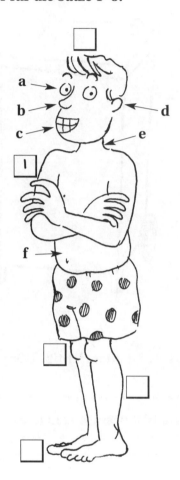

## B 📖 Du bist dran! Schreib weitere Sätze mit den Bildern a–f.

a   <u>Meine Augen tun weh!</u>

b   _____

c   _____

d   _____

e   _____

f   _____

**C1** Wo tut es weh? Schreib die Wörter auf.

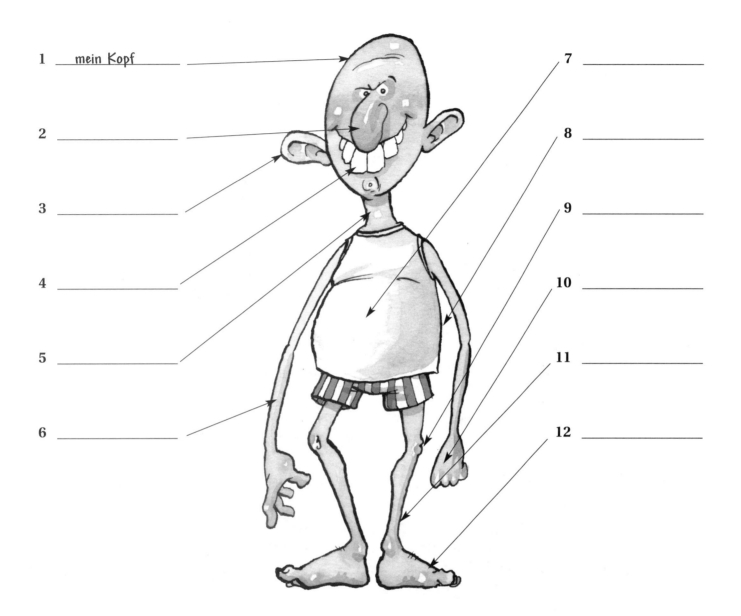

1   mein Kopf

2   _____

3   _____

4   _____

5   _____

6   _____

7   _____

8   _____

9   _____

10   _____

11   _____

12   _____

**C2** Ist alles richtig? A sagt eine Zahl (ein Bild) von Übung C1, B antwortet.

*Beispiel:*

A   *Nummer 1 – wo tut es weh?*

B   *Mein Kopf! Mein Kopf tut weh!*

**D** „Ich habe …schmerzen!" Was sagen sie? Schreib Sprechblasen.

a

Ich habe Kopfschmerzen!

c

b

d

**E1** Beim Arzt – finde die richtige Reihenfolge für den Dialog.

a  Seit gestern. ☐

b  Ja, ich habe auch Husten. ☐

c  Ich habe Fieber. ☐

d  Guten Morgen! Was fehlt dir? ☐ 1

e  Hast du auch Husten? ☐

f  Seit wann hast du Fieber? ☐

**E2** 🔊 Ist alles richtig? Hör gut zu.

**F** „Was fehlt dir?" Finde die passenden Bilder.

1  Ich habe Fieber. ☐

2  Ich habe Husten. ☐

3  Ich habe Grippe. ☐

4  Ich habe Heuschnupfen. ☐

5  Ich habe Schnupfen. ☐

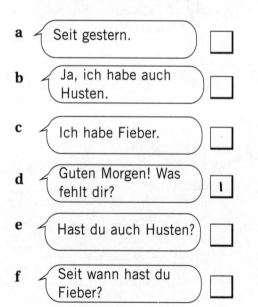

**G** 🔊 **Was sagt der Arzt? Hör gut zu und finde die passenden Bilder.**

a    b    c    d    e

☐    **2/T** ☐    |  **1/T** ☐    **3/T** ☐    **3/T** ☐

**H** 👥👥 **Beim Arzt – macht Dialoge mit den Informationen.**

*Beispiel:*

A   *Was fehlt dir?*

B   *Ich habe Grippe. Und ich habe Halsschmerzen.*

A   *Seit wann hast du Grippe?*

B   *Seit Samstag.*

1   Grippe, Hals seit Samstag

2   Kopf + Husten seit zwei Tagen

3   Bauch, Fieber seit einer Woche

4   Ohren, Schnupfen seit drei Tagen

5   Heuschnupfen, Augen seit Dienstag

**I1 Tina muss am Samstag zu Hause bleiben. Lies die Nachricht an Tinas Freundin und füll die Lücken aus.**

Hallo Kim!

Ich kann heute leider nicht _____

_____ gehen . Ich habe

seit _____   M D M D F S S / 5 6 7 8 9 10 11

Husten und ich habe seit

M D M D / 5 6 7 8   _____

. Und mein

_____

tut weh!

**I2 Schreib eine weitere Nachricht mit den Informationen unten.**

_____
_____
_____
_____
_____
_____
_____
_____
_____

**J**  **Was isst du zum Frühstück? Schreib die Wörter auf.**

**K1** **Finde 14 Essen- und Trinken-Wörter und schreib sie auf.**

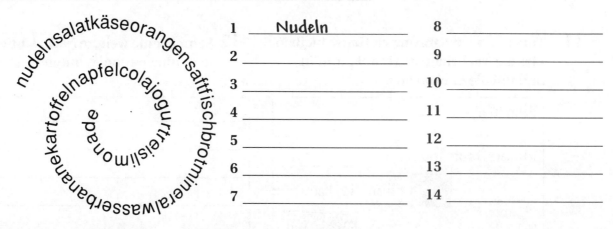

1  Nudeln

2  _____

3  _____

4  _____

5  _____

6  _____

7  _____

8  _____

9  _____

10  _____

11  _____

12  _____

13  _____

14  _____

**K2** **Finde dann die passenden Bilder für die Wörter in Übung K1.**

**L1** Was isst Sven gern? Füll die Lücken aus.

1

P__ __z__

2

H__h__ __he__

3

S__ho__ __la__e

4

P__ __me__ f__ __ __e__

5

Cu__ __yw__r__ __

6

H__ __b__ __ger

7

Ei__ m__ __ S__ __ne

8

K__ __t__ __f__ls__ l__t

9

C__ __ __s

**L2** [icon] Was isst du gern? Macht Dialoge mit den Bildern von Übung L1.

*Beispiel:*

A   *Ich esse gern Pizza. Und du? Was isst du gern?*

B   *Ich esse gern …*

**M1** Lies noch einmal die Essen- und Trinken-Wörter in Übung J–L. Was meinst du – was ist sehr gesund, ziemlich gesund oder ungesund? Schreib die Wörter auf.

| sehr gesund | ziemlich gesund | ungesund |
|---|---|---|
|  |  |  |
|  |  |  |
|  |  |  |
|  |  |  |
|  |  |  |

**M2** Was sagt dein Partner/deine Partnerin? Macht Dialoge.

*Beispiel:*

A  *Müsli ist sehr gesund, finde ich.*

B  *Ja, das stimmt! Und Kaffee ist …*

**N1** Was machen Anne und Thomas für ihre Gesundheit? Hör gut zu und schreib A (Anne) oder T (Thomas) auf.

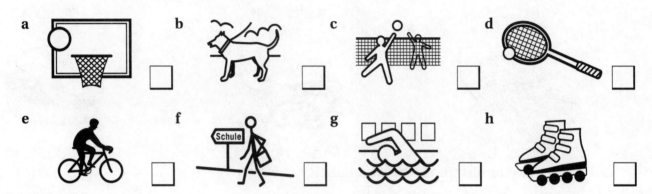

a ☐  b ☐  c ☐  d ☐

e ☐  f ☐  g ☐  h ☐

**N2** „Was machst du für die Gesundheit?" Macht Dialoge.

*Beispiel:*

A  *Was machst du für die Gesundheit?*

B  *Ich spiele Golf. Und du? Was machst du für die Gesundheit?*

A  *Ich …*

**N3** Du bist dran! Wie oft/seit wann machst du das? Schreib Sätze mit den Wörtern.

| jeden Tag | seit zwei Jahren | zweimal pro Woche |
|---|---|---|
| seit sechs Monaten | jeden Abend | jedes Wochenende |

_____

_____

_____

_____

**O1** Schreib die Sätze richtig auf.

1 Wasser viel Trink ! _____

2 nicht Rauch ! _____

3 viel Iss Gemüse ! _____

4 zu viel Fuß Geh ! _____

5 Süßigkeiten keine Iss ! _____

6 keinen Trink Alkohol ! _____

7 Sport viel Mach ! _____

8 kein Iss Fastfood ! _____

**O2** Finde die passenden Bilder für die Sätze in Übung O1.

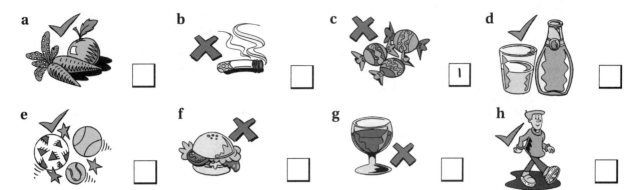

a    ☐    b    ☐    c    1    d    ☐

e    ☐    f    ☐    g    ☐    h    ☐

**O3** 📼 Ist alles richtig? Hör gut zu.

**O4** Schreib weitere Tipps für die Gesundheit.

a

_____

_____

b

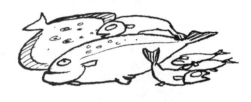

_____

_____

c

_____

_____

d

_____

_____

**P** 👥 Welche Tipps in Übung O findest du gut/wichtig? Warum?
Macht Dialoge mit deinem Partner/deiner Partnerin.

*Beispiel:*

A   *Rauch nicht! Das finde ich gut. Rauchen ist nicht gesund! Und du?*

B   *Iss kein …*

**Q** 📼 Was soll man für die Gesundheit tun? Hör gut zu und finde die passenden Bilder.

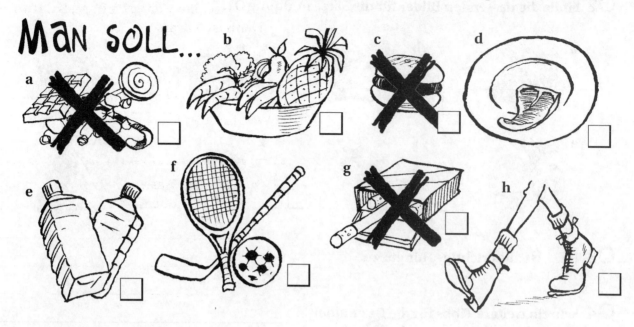

MaN SoLL...

a

b

c

d

e

f

g

h

---

**R** Schreib Sprechblasen für die Bilder.

a
> Man soll keine Cola trinken.

b

c

d

e

f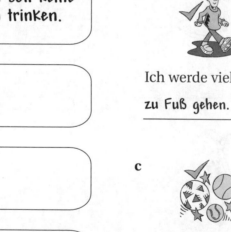

**S** Matthias will im neuen Jahr viel für die Gesundheit tun. Füll die Lücken aus.

a  b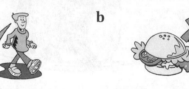

Ich werde viel

zu Fuß gehen.

Ich werde kein

_____

_____ .

c  d

Ich werde viel _____

_____ .

Ich werde _____

_____

_____ .

e  f

_____

_____ _____

_____ .

**T1** Was willst du im neuen Jahr für die Gesundheit tun? Schreib Sätze für dein Tagebuch.

1 _Ich werde..._

2 _____

3 _____

4 _____

5 _____

6 _____

1
2
3
4
5
6

**T2** Ist alles richtig? A fragt, B antwortet. Dann ist B dran.

*Beispiel:*

**A** *Was willst du im neuen Jahr für die Gesundheit tun? Bild 1!*

**B** *Ich werde …*

**U** Du bist dran! Was willst du im neuen Jahr für die Gesundheit tun?

_____
_____
_____
_____
_____
_____
_____
_____
_____
_____
_____
_____

| Can you …? | Listening | Speaking | Reading | Writing |
|---|---|---|---|---|
| name parts of your body | | | | |
| ask someone what's wrong | | | | |
| say where it hurts | | | | |
| ask how long someone's been ill | | | | |
| say how long you've been ill | | | | |
| understand the doctor's instructions | | | | |
| understand and discuss what's good/bad for your health | | | | |
| say what you do for your health | | | | |
| understand and give advice on healthy eating | | | | |
| say what you should or shouldn't do for a healthy lifestyle | | | | |
| say what you're going to do for your health in future | | | | |

# 9 Zukunft

**A**   **Schreib die Sätze richtig auf.**

1   viel | Ich | faulenzen | werde | . _____

2   Ausflug | machen | wird | Katja | einen | . _____

3   ins | Kino | gehen | werden | Wir | . _____

4   spielen | Tennis | wird | Martin | . _____

5   werden | Wir | Italien | fahren | nach | . _____

6   Oma | Ich | besuchen | meine | werde | . _____

**B 1**  **Was machst du in den Sommerferien? Finde die passenden Sätze für die Bilder.**

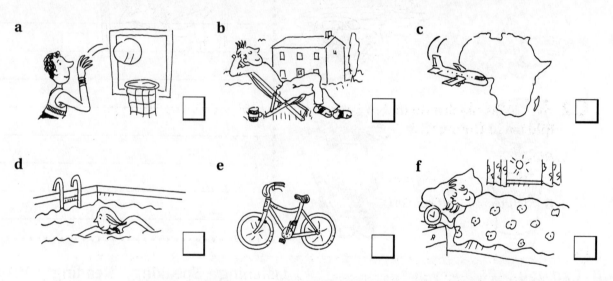

a          b          c

d          e          f

1   Ich werde eine Radtour machen.          4   Ich werde lange schlafen.

2   Wir werden ins Schwimmbad gehen.        5   Wir werden Basketball spielen.

3   Thomas wird zu Hause bleiben.           6   Susi wird nach Afrika fliegen.

**B 2**  **Ratespiel: A spielt ein Bild von Übung B1 und fragt,
B antwortet. Dann ist B dran.**

*Beispiel:*

*A   Was machst du in den Sommerferien? (spielt „Ich werde nach Afrika fliegen")*

*B   Bild c! Ich werde nach Afrika fliegen.*

**C1** 🔊 **Was machen Sarah und Carsten in den Sommerferien? Hör gut zu und schreib S (Sarah) oder C (Carsten) auf.**

**C2** 👥 **„Was machst du in den Sommerferien?" Macht Dialoge mit den Bildern in Übung C1.**

*Biespiel:*

**A** *Was machst du in den Sommerferien?*

**B** *Ich werde Golf spielen.*

**D** **Was machen Sven, Atalay, Jasmin und Annika in den Ferien? Lies Svens Postkarte und füll die Lücken aus.**

| wird | werden | werde | wirst | wird | werden |

Hallo Uwe!

Was _____ du in den Sommerferien machen? Ich

_____ meine Eltern in Chemnitz besuchen. Meine

Schwester und ich – wir _____ dort viel faulenzen. Und

Jasmin? Jasmin _____ zu Hause bleiben – und Atalay

auch. Sie _____ einen Skateboardkurs machen! Und

Annika _____ eine Radtour machen.

**E1**   Lies Susis E-Mail und füll die Lücken aus.

| gehen | besuchen | machen |
|-------|----------|--------|
| spielen | fliegen | machen |

Hallo Kathi!

Was machst du in den Sommerferien? Ich werde Urlaub in Spanien _____ - zwei Wochen lang! Ich werde nach Valencia _____ und ich werde dort meine Brieffreundin Pilar _____ . Wir werden auch einen Ausflug nach Madrid _____ . Ach ja, und wir werden auch ins Popkonzert _____ - super! Und am Wochenende werde ich mit Pilar Volleyball _____ - am Strand!

**E2**  Was macht Tobias in den Sommerferien? Schreib eine E-Mail-Nachricht (so wie Susi) mit den Bildern.

**F**   Du bist dran! Was machst du in den Sommerferien?

**G** 🔊 Jasmin und Sven wollen im neuen Schuljahr viel für die Schule tun.
Hör gut zu und schreib *J* (Jasmin) oder *S* (Sven) auf.

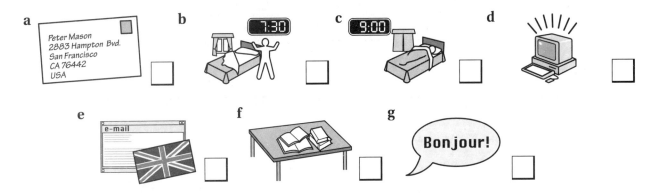

**H** Was will Daniel im neuen Schuljahr tun? Schreib Sprechblasen.

**a** Ich werde um 7 Uhr aufstehen.

**b** Guten Tag! Hallo!

**f** E-Mail Hi Daniel!

**I** 👥 „Was willst du im neuen Schuljahr für die Schule tun?"
Macht Dialoge mit den Bildern von Übung G und H.

*Beispiel:*

*A   Was willst du im neuen Schuljahr für die Schule tun?*

*B   Ich werde um 7 Uhr aufstehen. Und du?*

*A   Ich werde …*

**J** Du bist dran! Was willst du im neuen Schuljahr für die Schule tun?

_____

_____

_____

_____

**K** Finde die passenden Bilder.

1 Dieses Jahr habe ich Nähen gewählt.
  Nächstes Jahr werde ich Werken wählen.

2 Dieses Jahr habe ich eine Umwelt-AG gemacht.
  Nächstes Jahr werde ich einen Computerkurs machen.

3 Dieses Jahr habe ich Klavier gelernt.
  Nächstes Jahr werde ich Gitarre lernen.

a ☐

b ☐

c ☐

**L** Was haben sie dieses Jahr gemacht? Was wollen sie nächstes Jahr machen? Füll die Sprechblasen aus.

a

Dieses Jahr _____ _____ _____ gewählt. Nächstes Jahr werde ich _____ _____ .

b

_____ _____ _____ _____ gemacht. Nächstes Jahr _____ _____ _____ machen.

c

_____ _____ _____ . _____ _____ .

**M** 🗣 **Was hast du dieses Jahr gemacht? Was willst du nächstes Jahr machen? Macht Dialoge mit den Informationen.**

*Beispiel:*

**A** *Dieses Jahr habe ich Fußball gemacht. Nächstes Jahr werde ich Tennis machen. Und du?*

**B** *Dieses Jahr …*

Basketball — Werken — Volleyball — Computerkurs — Fußball — Nähen — Geige — Gitarre — Klavier — Tennis — Theater-AG — Kochkurs — Umwelt-AG

**N** **Sieh auch Lehrbuch, Seite 113. Lies die Sätze und füll die Lücken aus.**

**Präsens**

Ich **mache** Hausaufgaben.

Ich **gehe** in die Disco.

**Perfekt**

Ich _____ Hausaufgaben _____ .

Ich _____ in die Disco _____ .

**Futur**

Ich _____ Hausaufgaben _____ .

Ich _____ in die Disco _____ .

**O1** **Was hast du am Wochenende gemacht? Was machst du heute? Und was wirst du nächste Woche machen? Schreib eine Postkarte mit den Bildern.**

am Wochenende:

heute:

nächste Woche:

----------------------------------------

**O2** **Du bist dran! Was hast du am Wochenende gemacht? Was machst du heute? Und was wirst du nächste Woche machen? Mach eine Kassette mit deinen Informationen.**

**P1** Was ist er/sie von Beruf? Schreib die passenden Wörter auf.

a   b   c   d

<u>Krankenpfleger</u>      _____      _____      _____

e   f   g   h

_____      _____      _____      _____

**P2** Ⓦ▯ Schreib die passenden Maskulinum- und Femininum-Formen
für die Wörter in Übung P1 auf.

| | Maskulinum | Femininum |
|---|---|---|
| a | Krankenpfleger | Krankenschwester |
| b | _____ | _____ |
| c | _____ | _____ |
| d | _____ | _____ |
| e | _____ | _____ |
| f | _____ | _____ |
| g | _____ | _____ |
| h | _____ | _____ |

**P3** 👥 Ratespiel: „Was ist dein Vater/deine Mutter von Beruf?" A buchstabiert
einen Beruf, B antwortet. Dann ist B dran.

*Beispiel:*

**A** *Was ist dein Vater von Beruf? K–*

**B** *Krankenpfleger!*

**A** *Nein! K–E …*

**Q** 🔊 **Was möchten sie werden? Hör gut zu und finde die richtige Reihenfolge für die Berufe.**

a ☐

b ☐

c ☐

d ☐

e ☐

f ☐

g ☐

h ☐

**R** „Ich möchte … werden" – was sagen diese Schüler/Schülerinnen? Schreib Sätze für sie.

Ute    Tim    Ina    Heiko    Sandra    Anne    Olli    Jens

Ute: _____Ich möchte Ärztin werden._____

Tim: _____

Ina: _____

Heiko: _____

Sandra: _____

Anne: _____

Olli: _____

Jens: _____

**S**  **Du bist dran! Was möchtest du später werden?**

_____

_____

**T**  **Was möchte Leah später gern machen? Finde die passenden Bilder.**

**Ich möchte später gern …**

1  ein schönes Auto kaufen.  ☐

2  jedes Wochenende eine Party machen.  ☐

3  jeden Abend im Restaurant essen.  ☐

4  Popstar werden.  ☐

5  viele Geschenke für meine Familie kaufen.  ☐

6  eine große Wohnung haben.  ☐

a

b

c

d

e

f

**U 1** 🔊 **Was möchten Svenja und Tobias später gern machen? Hör gut zu und schreib *S* (Svenja) oder *T* (Tobias) auf.**

**U 2** 👥 **Was möchtest du später gern machen? A fragt und wählt ein Bild, B antwortet. Dann ist B dran.**

*Beispiel:*

**A**   *Was möchtest du später gern machen?*
    *Bild a!*

**B**   *Ich möchte im Ausland arbeiten!*

**V**   **Du bist dran! Was möchtest du später gern machen?**

_____

_____

_____

_____

| Can you …? | Listening | Speaking | Reading | Writing |
|---|---|---|---|---|
| ask others about their plans for the holidays | | | | |
| talk about your plans for the holidays | | | | |
| talk about other people's plans for the holidays | | | | |
| talk about resolutions for the new academic year | | | | |
| compare this year and next year | | | | |
| ask what someone else's parents do | | | | |
| say what jobs your parents do | | | | |
| talk about your future job plans | | | | |
| talk about what you would like to do in the future | | | | |

# Notizen